李斯列傳第二十七

李斯者楚上蔡人也索隱曰地理志汝南有上蔡縣云古蔡國周武王弟叔度所封至十八代平侯徙新蔡二蔡皆屬汝南後二代至昭侯徙上蔡屬沛六國時爲楚地故曰楚上蔡也年少時爲
郡小吏索隱曰郡一作鄉劉氏云掌鄉內文書見吏舍廁中鼠食不
潔近人犬數驚恐之斯入倉觀倉中鼠食積粟
居大廡之下不見人犬之憂於是李斯乃歎曰
人之賢不肖譬如鼠矣在所自處耳乃從荀卿
學帝王之術學已成度楚王不足事而六國皆
弱無可爲建功者欲西入秦辭於荀卿曰斯聞
得時無怠今萬乘方爭時游者主事索隱曰言萬乘爭雄之時

存說者可以立功成名當得典主事務也劉氏云游歷諸侯當見彊主以事之於文紆迴非也今秦王欲
吞天下稱帝而治此布衣馳騖之時而游說者
之秋也正義曰言秋時萬物成孰今爭彊時亦說士成孰時處卑賤之位而計
不爲者此禽鹿視肉人面而能彊行者耳索隱曰禽鹿猶禽獸也言禽獸但知視肉而食之莊子及蘇子曰人而不學譬之視肉而食揚子法言曰人而不學如禽何言不暇游說取榮貴即如禽獸徒有人面而能彊行也故詬莫大於卑賤正義曰呼后反耻辱也
而悲莫甚於窮困久處卑賤之位困苦之地非
世而惡利正義曰言譏世富貴惡其榮利自託於無爲者非士人之情實力不能致此也自託
於無爲此非士之情也索隱曰非者譏也所謂處士橫議之時也故斯
將西說秦王矣至秦會莊襄王卒李斯乃求

爲秦相文信侯呂不韋舍人不韋賢之任以爲郎李斯因以得說說秦王曰胥人者去其幾也索隱曰胥人猶胥吏小人也去猶失也幾者動之微以言君子見幾而作不俟終日小人不識動微之會故每失時也劉氏解幾爲釁非也○正義曰胥相也幾謂察也言關東六國與秦相敵者君臣機密並有瑕釁可成大功而遂忍之成大功者在因瑕釁而遂忍之索隱曰言因諸侯有瑕釁則忍心而翦除故我將說秦以并天下也昔者秦穆公之霸終不東并六國者何也諸侯尚衆周德未衰故五伯迭興更尊周室自秦孝公以來周室卑微諸侯相兼關東爲六國秦之乘勝役諸侯蓋六世矣正義曰秦孝公惠王文武王昭王孝文王莊襄王今諸侯服秦譬若郡縣夫以秦之彊大

王之賢由竈上騷除徐廣曰騷音掃○索隱曰言秦欲并天下若炊婦掃除竈上之不淨不足爲難也足以滅諸侯成帝業爲天下一統此萬世之一時也今怠而不急就諸侯復彊相聚約從雖有黃帝之賢不能并也秦王乃拜斯爲長史聽其計陰遣謀士齎持金玉以游說諸侯諸侯名士可下以財者厚遺結之不肯者利劍刺之離其君臣之計秦王乃使其良將隨其後秦王拜斯爲客卿會韓人鄭國來間秦以作注溉渠正義曰鄭國渠首起雍州雲陽縣西南二十五里自山邸口爲渠傍北山東注洛三百餘里以溉田又曰韓苦秦兵而使水工鄭國間秦作注溉渠令費人工不東伐也已而覺秦宗室大臣皆

言秦王曰諸矦人來事秦者大抵爲其主游間於秦耳請一切逐客索隱曰一切猶一例言盡逐之也言切者譬若利刀之割一運斤無不斷者解漢書者以一切爲權時義亦未爲得也李斯議亦在逐中斯乃上書曰正義曰在始皇十年臣聞吏議逐客竊以爲過矣昔繆公求士西取由余於戎東得百里奚於宛索隱曰秦本紀云晉獻公以百里奚爲秦穆公夫人媵於秦奚亡走宛楚鄙人執之是也○正義曰新序云百里奚楚宛人仕於虞虞亡入秦號五羖大夫也迎蹇叔於宋索隱曰秦紀又云百里奚謂穆公曰臣不如臣友蹇叔蹇叔賢而世莫知穆公厚幣迎之以爲上大夫今云於宋未詳所出○正義曰括地志云蹇叔岐州人也時游宋故迎之於宋求丕豹公孫支於晉索隱曰丕豹自晉奔秦左氏傳有明文公孫支所謂子桑也是秦大夫而云自晉以來亦未見其所出○正義曰括地志云公孫支岐州人遊晉後歸秦此五者不

產於秦而繆公用之并國二十遂霸西戎索隱曰秦本紀穆公用由余謀伐戎王益國十二開地千里遂霸西戎此都言五子之功故云并國二十或易爲十二誤也孝公用商鞅之法移風易俗民以殷盛國以富彊百姓樂用諸矦親服獲楚魏之師舉地千里至今治彊惠王用張儀之計拔三川之地西并巴蜀索隱曰案惠王時張儀爲相請伐韓下兵三川以臨二周司馬錯請伐蜀惠王從之果滅蜀儀死後武王欲通車三川令甘茂拔宜陽今並云張儀者以儀爲秦相雖錯滅蜀甘茂通三川皆歸功於相又三川是儀先請伐故也北收上郡正義曰惠王十年魏納上郡十五縣南取漢中正義曰惠王十三年攻楚漢中取地六百里包九夷制鄢郢索隱曰九夷即屬楚之夷也地理志南郡江陵縣云故楚郢都又宜城縣云故鄢也○正義曰夷謂并巴蜀收上都取漢中伐義渠丹犂是也九夷本東夷九種此言者文體然也東據

成皋之險正義曰河南府汜水縣也割膏腴之壤遂散六國之從使之西面事秦功施到今昭王得范雎廢穰侯逐華陽徐廣曰華一作葉彊公室杜私門蠶食諸侯使秦成帝業索隱曰高誘注淮南云蠶食盡無餘也此四君者皆以客之功由此觀之客何負於秦哉向使四君却客而不內疏士而不用是使國無富利之實而秦無彊大之名也今陛下致昆山之玉正義曰昆岡在于闐國東北四百里其岡出玉有隨和之寶正義曰括地志云濆山一名崑山一名斷蛇丘在隨州隨縣北二十五里說苑云昔隨侯行遇大蛇中斷疑其靈使人以藥封之蛇乃能去因號其處爲斷蛇丘歲餘蛇銜明珠徑寸絕白而有光因號隨珠卞和璧始皇以爲傳國璽也垂明月之珠服太阿之

劒見蘇秦傳乘纖離之馬徐廣曰纖離蒲稍皆駿馬名○索隱曰徐氏據孫卿子而爲說建翠鳳之旗樹靈鼉之鼓鄭玄注月令云鼉皮可以冒鼓此數寶者秦不生一焉而陛下說之何也必秦國之所生然後可則是夜光之璧不飾朝廷犀象之器不爲玩好鄭衛之女不充後宮而駿良駃騠不實外廄索隱曰駃音決騠音提周書曰正北以駃騠爲獻廣雅曰馬屬也郭景純注上林賦云生三日而超其母也江南金錫不爲用西蜀丹青不爲采所以飾後宮充下陳索隱曰下陳猶後列也晏子曰有二女願得入身於下陳是也娛心意說耳目者必出於秦然後可則是宛珠之簪傅璣之珥索隱曰宛音於阮反傅音附即隨珠也宛者謂以珠宛轉而裝其簪傅者以璣附著於珥珥者瑱也璣是

珠之不圓者或云宛珠宛地之珠也隨在漢水之南宛亦近漢故曰宛珠璣者女飾也言女傅之珥以璣爲之並非秦所有物也阿縞之衣錦繡之飾徐廣曰齊之東阿縣繒帛所出不進於前而隨俗雅化徐廣曰隨俗一作脩使○索隱曰謂閑雅變化而能隨俗也佳冶窈窕趙女不立於側也夫擊甕叩缻彈箏搏髀而歌呼嗚嗚快耳目者眞秦之聲也索隱曰說文云甕汲缻也音於貢反缶瓦器也秦人鼓之以節樂缻音甫有反鄭衛桑間昭虞武象者索隱曰昭作韶異國之樂也今棄擊甕叩缻而就鄭衛退彈箏而取昭虞若是者何也快意當前適觀而已矣今取人則不然不問可否不論曲直非秦者去爲客者逐然則是所重者在乎色樂珠玉

而所輕者在乎人民也此非所以跨海內制諸侯之術也臣聞地廣者粟多國大者人衆兵彊則士勇是以太山不讓土壤故能成其大河海不擇細流故能就其深王者不却衆庶故能明其德索隱曰管子曰海不辭水故能成其大泰山不辭土石故能成其高文子曰聖人不讓負薪之言以廣其名也是以地無四方民無異國四時充美鬼神降福此五帝三王之所以無敵也今乃棄黔首以資敵國索隱曰資猶給也却賓客以業諸侯使天下之士退而不敢西向裹足不入秦此所謂藉寇兵而齎盜糧者也索隱曰藉音積夜反齎音子奚反說文曰齎持遺也齎或爲資義亦通夫

物不產於秦可寶者多士不產於秦而願忠者衆今逐客以資敵國損民以益讎內自虛而外樹怨於諸侯求國無危不可得也秦王乃除逐客之令復李斯官（新序曰斯在逐中道上上諫書達始皇始皇使人逐至驪邑得還）卒用其計謀官至廷尉二十餘年竟并天下尊主爲皇帝以斯爲丞相夷郡縣城銷其兵刃示不復用使秦無尺土之封不立子弟爲王功臣爲諸侯者使後無戰攻之患始皇三十四年置酒咸陽宮博士僕射周青臣等頌稱始皇威德齊人淳于越進諫曰臣聞之殷周之王千餘歲封

子弟功臣自爲支輔今陛下有海內而子弟爲匹夫卒有田常六卿之患臣無輔弼何以相救哉事不師古而能長久者非所聞也今青臣等又面諛以重陛下過非忠臣也（索隱曰重音逐用反重者再也）始皇下其議丞相丞相謬其說絀其辭乃上書曰古者天下散亂莫能相一是以諸侯並作語皆道古以害今飾虛言以亂實人善其所私學以非上所建立今陛下并有天下辨白黑而定一尊（索隱曰劉氏云前時國異政家殊俗人造私語莫辨其真今乃分別白黑也秦始皇并六國定天下海內共尊立一帝故云定一尊）而私學乃相與非法教之制聞令下即

各以其私學議之入則心非出則巷議非主以爲名異趣以爲高率群下以造謗如此不禁則主勢降乎上黨與成乎下禁之便臣請諸有文學詩書百家語者蠲除去之令到滿三十日弗去黥爲城旦所不去者醫藥卜筮種樹之書若有欲學者以吏爲師始皇可其議收去詩書百家之語以愚百姓使天下無以古非今明法度定律令皆以始皇起同文書（正義曰六國制令不同今令同之）治離宮別館周徧天下明年又巡狩外攘四夷斯皆有力焉斯長男由爲三川守諸男皆尚秦公

主女悉嫁秦諸公子三川守李由告歸咸陽李斯置酒於家百官長皆前爲壽門廷車騎以千數李斯喟然而歎曰嗟乎吾聞之荀卿曰物禁太盛夫斯乃上蔡布衣閭巷之黔首上不知其駑下遂擢至此當今人臣之位無居臣上者可謂富貴極矣物極則衰吾未知所稅駕也（索隱曰稅駕猶解駕言休息也李斯言己今日富貴已極然未知向後吉凶止泊在何處也）始皇三十七年十月行出游會稽並海上北抵琅邪（正義曰今沂州）丞相斯中車府令趙高兼行符璽令事皆從始皇有二十餘子長子扶蘇以數直諫上上使監兵

上郡正義曰上郡故城在綏州上縣東南五十里蒙恬爲將少子胡亥
愛請從上許之餘子莫從辯士隱姓名遺秦將章邯書曰李斯爲秦王死廢十
七兄而立今王也然則二世是秦始皇第十八子此書在善文中其年七月始皇帝至
沙丘正義曰沙丘臺在邢州病甚令趙高爲書賜公子扶蘇
曰以兵屬蒙恬與喪會咸陽而葬書已封未授
使者始皇崩書及璽皆在趙高所獨子胡亥丞
相李斯趙高及幸宦者五六人知始皇崩餘羣
臣皆莫知也李斯以爲上在外崩無眞太子故
祕之置始皇居轀輬車中徐廣曰一作轀車百官奏事上
食如故宦者輒從轀輬車中可諸奏事文頴曰轀輬車

如今喪轜車也孟康曰如衣車有窗牖閉之則温開之則凉故名之轀輬車也如淳曰轀輬車其形廣大有羽飾也趙
高因留所賜扶蘇璽書而謂公子胡亥曰上崩
無詔封王諸子而獨賜長子書長子至即立爲
皇帝而子無尺寸之地爲之奈何胡亥曰固也
吾聞之明君知臣明父知子父捐命不封諸子
何可言者趙高曰不然方今天下之權存亡在子
與高及丞相耳願子圖之且夫臣人與見臣於
人制人與見制於人豈可同日道哉胡亥曰廢
兄而立弟是不義也不奉父詔而畏死是不孝
也能薄而材譾史記音隱宰顯反○索隱曰劉氏音將淺反則譾亦淺義古人語自有重輕所

以文字有異

彊因人之功是不能也三者逆德天下不服身殆傾危社稷不血食高曰臣聞湯武殺其主天下稱義焉不爲不忠衛君殺其父而衛國載其德孔子著之不爲不孝夫大行不小謹盛德不辭讓鄉曲各有宜而百官不同功胡顧小而忘大後必有害狐疑猶豫後必有悔斷而敢行鬼神避之後有成功願子遂之胡亥喟然歎曰今大行未發喪禮未終豈宜以此事干丞相哉趙高曰時乎時乎間不及謀贏糧躍馬唯恐後時胡亥既然高之言高曰不與丞相謀恐事

不能成臣請爲子與丞相謀之高乃謂丞相斯曰上崩賜長子書與喪會咸陽而立爲嗣書未行今上崩未有知者也所賜長子書及符璽皆在胡亥所定太子在君矦與高之口耳事將何如斯曰安得亡國之言此非人臣所當議也高曰君矦自料能孰與蒙恬功高孰與蒙恬謀遠不失孰與蒙恬無怨於天下孰與蒙恬長子舊而信之孰與蒙恬斯曰此五者皆不及蒙恬而君責之何深也高曰高固內官之廝役也幸得以刀筆之文進入秦宮管事二十餘年未嘗見

秦免罷丞相功臣有封及二世者也卒皆以誅
亡皇帝二十餘子皆君之所知長子剛毅而武
勇信人而奮士即位必用蒙恬爲丞相君侯終
不懷通侯之印歸於鄉里明矣高受詔教習胡
亥使學以法事數年矣未嘗見過失慈仁篤厚
輕財重士辯於心而詘於口盡禮敬士秦之諸
子未有及此者可以爲嗣君計而定之斯曰君
其反位斯奉主之詔聽天之命何慮之可定也
高曰安可危也危可安也安危不定何以貴聖
斯曰斯上蔡閭巷布衣也上幸擢爲丞相封爲

通侯子孫皆至尊位重祿者故將以存亡安危
屬臣也豈可負哉夫忠臣不避死而庶幾索隱曰斯
言忠臣之節本不避死言己今日亦庶幾盡忠不避死也孝子不勤勞而見危人
臣各守其職而已矣君其勿復言將令斯得罪
高曰蓋聞聖人遷徙無常就變而從時見末而
知本觀指而覩歸物固有之安得常法哉方今
天下之權命懸於胡亥高能得志焉且夫從外
制中謂之惑從下制上謂之賊故秋霜降者草
花落水搖動者萬物作索隱曰水搖者謂水洋而搖動也是春時而萬物皆生也
此必然之效也君何見之晚斯曰吾聞晉易太

子（正義曰謂廢申生立奚齊也）三世不安齊桓兄弟爭位（正義曰謂小白與公子糾）身死爲戮紂殺親戚（正義曰謂殺比干囚箕子）不聽諫者國爲丘墟遂危社稷三者逆天宗廟不血食斯其猶人哉安足爲謀（索隱曰言我今日猶是人人道守順豈能爲逆謀故文安足爲謀也）高曰上下合同可以長久中外若一事無表裏君聽臣之計即長有封侯世世稱孤必有喬松之壽孔墨之智今釋此而不從禍及子孫足以爲寒心善者因禍爲福君何處焉斯乃仰天而歎垂淚太息曰嗟乎獨遭亂世旣以不能死安託命哉於是斯乃聽高高乃報胡亥曰臣請

奉太子之明命以報丞相丞相斯敢不奉令於是乃相與謀詐爲受始皇詔丞相立子胡亥爲太子更爲書賜長子扶蘇曰朕巡天下禱祠名山諸神以延壽命今扶蘇與將軍蒙恬將師數十萬以屯邊十有餘年矣不能進而前士卒多耗無尺寸之功乃反數上書直言誹謗我所爲以不得罷歸爲太子日夜怨望扶蘇爲人子不孝其賜劍以自裁將軍恬與扶蘇居外不匡正宜知其謀爲人臣不忠其賜死以兵屬裨將王離封其書以皇帝璽遣胡亥客奉書賜扶蘇於

上郡使者至發書扶蘇泣入內舍欲自殺蒙恬止扶蘇曰陛下居外未立太子使臣將三十萬衆守邊公子爲監此天下重任也今一使者來即自殺安知其非詐請復請復請而後死未暮也使者數趣之扶蘇爲人仁謂蒙恬曰父而賜子死尚安復請即自殺蒙恬不肯死使者即以屬吏繫於陽周徐廣曰屬上郡○正義曰陽周寧州羅川縣之邑也使者還報胡亥斯高大喜至咸陽發喪太子立爲二世皇帝以趙高爲郎中令常侍中用事二世燕居乃召高與謀事謂曰夫人生居世間也譬猶騁六

驥過決隙也吾既已臨天下矣欲悉耳目之所好窮心志之所樂以安宗廟而樂萬姓長有天下終吾年壽其道可乎高曰此賢主之所能行也而昏亂主之所禁也臣請言之不敢避斧鉞之誅願陛下少留意焉夫沙丘之謀諸公子及大臣皆疑焉而諸公子盡帝兄大臣又先帝之所置也今陛下初立此其屬意怏怏皆不服恐爲變且蒙恬已死蒙毅將兵居外臣戰戰栗栗唯恐不終且陛下安得爲此樂乎二世曰爲之奈何趙高曰嚴法而刻刑令有罪者相坐誅至

收族滅大臣而遠骨肉貧者富之賤者貴之盡除去先帝之故臣更置陛下之所親信者近之此則陰德歸陛下害除而姦謀塞羣臣莫不被潤澤蒙厚德陛下則高枕肆志寵樂矣計莫出於此二世然高之言乃更爲法律於是羣臣諸公子有罪輒下高令鞠治之殺大臣蒙毅等公子十二人僇死咸陽市十公主矺死於杜（史記正義曰矺音貯格反○索隱曰矺音宅與磔同古今字異耳磔謂裂其支體而殺之）財物入於縣官相連坐者不可勝數公子高欲奔恐收族乃上書曰先帝無恙時臣入則賜食出則乘輿御府之

衣臣得賜之中廄之寶馬臣得賜之臣當從死而不能爲人子不孝爲人臣不忠不忠者無名以立於世臣請從死願葬酈山之足唯上幸哀憐之書上胡亥大說召趙高而示之曰此可謂急乎趙高曰人臣當憂死而不暇何變之得謀胡亥可其書賜錢十萬以葬法令誅罰日益刻深羣臣人人自危欲畔者衆又作阿房之宮治直馳道賦斂愈重戍傜無已於是楚戍卒陳勝吳廣等乃作亂起於山東傑俊相立自置爲侯王叛秦兵至鴻門而却李斯數欲請閒諫二世

不許而二世責問李斯曰吾有私議而有所聞於韓子也曰堯之有天下也堂高三尺采椽不斲徐廣曰采一名櫟一作柞○索隱曰采木名即今之櫟木也茅茨不翦雖逆旅之宿不勤於此矣冬日鹿裘夏日葛衣粢糲之食索隱曰粢音資糲音郎葛反粢者稷也糲者麁粟飯也藜藿之羹飯土匭徐廣曰一作溜啜土鉶音刑雖監門之養不觳於此矣徐廣曰觳音學觳一作轂推也○索隱曰爾雅云觳盡也言監門下人飯猶不盡此若徐氏云一作轂則字宜作較鄒氏音角禹鑿龍門通大夏疏九河曲九防正義曰謂河之九曲別為隄防決渟水致之海徐廣曰致一作放而股無胈胈膚毳皮脛無毛手足胼胝面目黎黑遂以死于外葬於會稽臣虜之

勞不烈於此矣然則夫所貴於有天下者豈欲苦形勞神身處逆旅之宿口食監門之養手持臣虜之作哉此不肖人之所勉也非賢者之所務也彼賢人之有天下也專用天下適己而已矣此所以貴於有天下也夫所謂賢人者必能安天下而治萬民今身且不能利將惡能治天下哉故吾願賜志廣欲長享天下而無害為之奈何李斯子由為三川守羣盜吳廣等西略地過去弗能禁章邯以破逐廣等兵使者覆案三川相屬誚讓斯居三公位如何令盜如此李斯

恐懼重爵祿不知所出乃阿二世意欲求容以書對曰夫賢主者必且能全道而行督責之術者也（索隱曰督者察也察其罪責之以刑罰也）督責之則臣不敢不竭能以徇其主矣此臣主之分定上下之義明則天下賢不肖莫敢不盡力竭任以徇其君矣是故主獨制於天下而無所制也能窮樂之極矣賢明之主也可不察焉故申子曰有天下而不恣睢（索隱曰恣音資二反睢音呼季反恣睢猶放縱也謂肆情縱恣也）命之曰以天下爲桎梏者（正義曰言有天下不能自縱恣督責乃勞身於天下若堯禹即以天下爲桎梏於身也）無他焉不能督責而顧以其身勞於天下之民

若堯禹然故謂之桎梏也夫不能修申韓之明術行督責之道專以天下自適也而徒務苦形勞神以身徇百姓則是黔首之役非畜天下者也何足貴哉夫以人徇己則己貴而人賤以己徇人則己賤而人貴故徇人者賤而人所徇者貴自古及今未有不然者也凡古之所爲尊賢者爲其貴也而所爲惡不肖者爲其賤也而堯禹以身徇天下者也因隨而尊之則亦失所爲尊賢之心矣夫可謂大繆矣謂之爲桎不亦宜乎不能督責之過也故韓子曰慈母有敗子而

嚴家無格虜者何也索隱曰格彊悍也虜奴隸也言嚴整之家本無格悍奴僕也則能罰之加焉必也故商君之法刑棄灰於道者正義曰棄灰於道者黥也韓子云殷之法棄灰於衢者刑子貢以爲重問之仲尼曰灰棄於衢必燔人必怒怒則鬭鬭則三族雖刑之可也夫棄灰薄罪也而被刑重罰也彼唯明主爲能深督輕罪夫罪輕且督深而況有重罪乎故民不敢犯也是故韓子曰布帛尋常庸人不釋索隱曰尋常以言其少也庸人弗釋者謂庸人見則取之不釋以其罪輕也故下云罰不必行則庸人弗釋尋常是也鑠金百鎰盜跖不搏者索隱曰爾雅云鑠美也言百鎰之美金在於地雖有盜跖之行亦不取者爲其財多而罪重也故下云搏必隨手刑盜跖不搏也搏猶攫也取也凡鳥翼擊物必轉足取攫故人取物亦云搏也非庸人之心重尋常之利深而盜跖之欲淺也又不以盜跖之行爲輕百鎰之重也搏必隨手刑則盜跖不搏百鎰而罰不必行也則庸人不釋尋常是故城高五丈而樓季不輕犯也許慎曰樓季魏文侯之弟王孫子曰樓季之兄也泰山之高百仞而跛牂牧其上詩云牂羊墳首毛傳曰牝曰牂夫樓季也而難五丈之限豈跛牂也而易百仞之高哉陗壍之勢異也索隱曰陗峻也高也音七笑反壍音漸以言峭峻則難登故樓季難五丈之限平壍則易涉故跛牂牧於泰山也明主聖王之所以能久處尊位長執重勢而獨擅天下之利者非有異道也能獨斷而審督責必深罰故天下不敢犯也今不務所以不

犯而事慈母之所以敗子也則亦不察於聖人之論矣夫不能行聖人之術則舍為天下役何事哉可不哀邪索隱曰舍猶廢也止也言為人主不能行聖人督責之術則廢止何為勤身苦心為天下所役是何哉可不哀邪言其非也且夫儉節仁義之人立於朝則荒肆之樂輟矣諫說論理之臣閒於側則流漫之志詘矣烈士死節之行顯於世則淫康之虞廢矣故明主能外此三者而獨操主術以制聽從之臣而脩其明法故身尊而勢重也凡賢主者必將能拂世摩俗而廢其所惡立其所欲索隱曰拂音扶弗反摩音莫何反拂世與世情乖戾摩俗言磨礪於俗使從己也故生則有尊

重之勢死則有賢明之謚也是以明君獨斷故權不在臣也然後能滅仁義之塗掩馳說之口困烈士之行塞聰揜明內獨視聽故外不可傾以仁義烈士之行而內不可奪以諫說忿爭之辯故能犖然獨行恣睢之心而莫之敢逆若此然後可謂能明申韓之術而脩商君之法法脩術明而天下亂者未之聞也故曰王道約而易操也唯明主為能行之若此則謂督責之誠則臣無邪臣無邪則天下安天下安則主嚴尊主嚴尊則督責必督責必則所求得所求得則國

家富國家富則君樂豐故督責之術設則所欲無不得矣羣臣百姓救過不給何變之敢圖若此則帝道備而可謂能明君臣之術矣雖申韓復生不能加也書奏二世悅於是行督責益嚴稅民深者爲明吏二世曰若此則可謂能督責矣刑者相半於道而死人日成積於市殺人衆者爲忠臣二世曰若此則可謂能督矣初趙高爲郎中令所殺及報私怨衆多恐大臣入朝奏事毀惡之乃說二世曰天子所以貴者但以聞聲羣臣莫得見其面故號曰朕且陛下富於春

秋未必盡通諸事徐廣曰通或且作照今坐朝廷譴舉有不當者則見短於大臣非所以示神明於天下也且陛下深拱禁中與臣及侍中習法者待事事來有以揆之徐廣曰揆一作撥也如此則大臣不敢奏疑事天下稱聖主矣二世用其計乃不坐朝廷見大臣居禁中趙高常侍中用事事皆決於趙高高聞李斯以爲言乃見丞相曰關東羣盜多今上急發繇治阿房宮索隱曰房音旁一如字聚狗馬無用之物臣欲諫爲位賤此眞君侯之事君何不諫李斯曰固也吾欲言之久矣今時上不坐朝廷上居

深宮吾有所言者不可傳也欲見無閒趙高謂
曰君誠能諫請爲君候上閒語君於是趙高待
二世方燕樂婦女居前使人告丞相上方閒可
奏事丞相至宮門上謁如此者三二世怒曰吾
常多閒日丞相不來吾方燕私丞相輒來請事
丞相豈少我哉且固我哉（索隱曰謂以我幼故輕我也一云固我者以我爲短小且固陋也於義爲踈）趙高因曰如此殆矣夫沙丘之謀丞
相與焉今陛下已立爲帝而丞相貴不益此其
意亦望裂地而王矣且陛下不問臣臣不敢言
丞相長男李由爲三川守楚盜陳勝等皆丞相

傍縣之子以故楚盜公行（徐廣曰公一作訟音私）過三川城
守不肯擊高聞其文書相往來未得其審故未
敢以聞且丞相居外權重於陛下二世以爲然
欲案丞相恐其不審乃使人案驗三川守與盜
通狀李斯聞之是時二世在甘泉方作觳抵優
俳之觀（應劭曰戰國之時稍增講武之禮以爲戲樂用相夸示而秦更名曰角抵角者角材也抵者相抵觸也文穎曰案秦名此樂爲角抵兩兩相當角力角伎藝射御故曰角抵也駰案觳抵即角抵）李斯不得
見因上書言趙高之短曰臣聞之臣疑其君無
不危國妾疑其夫無不危家今有大臣於陛下
擅利擅害與陛下無異此甚不便昔者司城子

罕相宋身行刑罰以威行之朞年遂刼其君田常為簡公臣爵列無敵於國私家之富與公家均布恵施德下得百姓上得羣臣陰取齊國殺宰予於庭即弒簡公於朝遂有齊國此天下所明知也今高有邪佚之志危反之行如子罕相宋也私家之富若田氏之於齊也兼行田常子罕之逆道而刼陛下之威信其志若韓玘為韓安相也索隱曰玘亦作起並音怡韓大夫弒其君悼公者然韓無悼公或鄭之嗣君案表韓玘事昭侯昭侯已下四代至王安其說非也陛下不圖臣恐其為變也二世曰何哉夫高故宦人也然不為安肆志不以危易

心潔行脩善自使至此以忠得進以信守位朕實賢之而君疑之何也且朕少失先人無所識知不習治民而君又老恐與天下絶矣朕非屬趙君當誰任哉且趙君為人精廉彊力下知人情上能適朕君其勿疑李斯曰不然夫高故賤人也無識於理貪欲無厭求利不止列勢次主求欲無窮臣故曰殆二世已前信趙高恐李斯殺之乃私告趙高高曰丞相所患者獨高高已死丞相即欲為田常所為於是二世曰其以李斯屬郎中令趙高案治李斯李斯拘執束縛居

囹圄中仰天而歎曰嗟乎悲夫不道之君何可
爲計哉昔者桀殺關龍逢紂殺王子比干吳王
夫差殺伍子胥此三臣者豈不忠哉然而不免
於死身死而所忠者非也今吾智不及三子而
二世之無道過於桀紂夫差吾以忠死宜矣且
二世之治豈不亂哉日者夷其兄弟而自立也
殺忠臣而貴賤人作爲阿房之宮賦斂天下吾
非不諫也而不吾聽也凡古聖王飲食有節車
器有數宮室有度出令造事加費而無益於民
利者禁故能長久治安今行逆於昆弟不顧其

咎侵殺忠臣不思其殃大爲宮室厚賦天下不
愛其費三者已行天下不聽今反者已有天下
之半矣而心尚未寤也而以趙高爲佐吾必見
寇至咸陽麋鹿游於朝也於是二世乃使高案
丞相獄治罪責斯與子由謀反狀皆收捕宗族
賓客趙高治斯榜掠千餘不勝痛自誣服斯所
以不死者自負其辯有功實無反心幸得上書
自陳幸二世之寤而赦之李斯乃從獄中上書
曰臣爲丞相治民三十餘年矣逮秦地之陝隘
先王之時秦地不過千里兵數十萬臣盡薄材

謹奉法令陰行謀臣資之金玉使游說諸侯陰
脩甲兵飾政教官鬬士尊功臣盛其爵祿故終
以脅韓弱魏破燕趙夷齊楚卒兼六國虜其王
立秦爲天子罪一矣地非不廣又北逐胡貉南
定百越以見秦之彊罪二矣尊大臣盛其爵位
以固其親罪三矣立社稷脩宗廟以明主之賢
罪四矣更剋畫平斗斛度量文章布之天下以
樹秦之名罪五矣治馳道興游觀以見主之得
意罪六矣緩刑罰薄賦斂以遂主得衆之心萬
民戴王死而不忘罪七矣若斯之爲臣者罪足

以死固久矣上幸盡其能力乃得至今願陛下
察之書上趙高使吏棄去不奏曰囚安得上書
趙高使其客十餘輩詐爲御史謁者侍中更往
覆訊斯斯更以其實對輒使人復榜之後二世
使人驗斯斯以爲如前終不敢更言辭服奏當
上二世喜曰微趙君幾爲丞相所賣及二世所
使案三川之守至則項梁已擊殺之使者來會
丞相下吏趙高皆妄爲反辭二世二年七月具
斯五刑論要斬咸陽市斯出獄與其中子俱執
顧謂其中子曰吾欲與若復牽黃犬俱出上蔡

東門逐狡兔豈可得乎遂父子相哭而夷三族
李斯已死二世拜趙高爲中丞相事無大小輒
決於高高自知權重乃獻鹿謂之馬二世問左
右此乃鹿也左右皆曰馬也二世驚自以爲惑
乃召太卜令卦之太卜曰陛下春秋郊祀奉宗
廟鬼神齋戒不明故至于此可依盛德而明齋
戒於是乃入上林齋戒日游弋獵有行人入上
林中二世自射殺之趙高教其女壻咸陽令閻
樂劾不知何人賊殺人移上林高乃諫二世曰
天子無故賊殺不辜人此上帝之禁也鬼神不

享天且降殃當遠避宮以禳之二世乃出居望
夷之宮留三日趙高詐詔衛士令士皆素服持
兵內鄉入告二世曰山東羣盜兵大至二世上
觀而見之恐懼高卽因劫令自殺引璽而佩之
左右百官莫從上殿殿欲壞者三高自知天弗
與羣臣弗許乃召始皇弟授之璽徐廣曰一本曰召始皇弟子嬰
授之璽秦本紀云子嬰者二世之兄子也○索隱曰劉氏云弟字誤當爲孫子嬰也子嬰卽位患
之乃稱疾不聽事與宦者韓談及其子謀殺高
高上謁請病因召入令韓談刺殺之夷其三族
子嬰立三月沛公兵從武關入至咸陽羣臣百

官皆畔不適徐廣曰適音敵也子嬰與妻子自係其頸以組降軹道旁正義曰軹道在萬年縣東北十六里沛公因以屬吏項王至而斬之遂以亡天下

太史公曰李斯以閭閻歷諸侯入事秦因以瑕釁以輔始皇卒成帝業斯爲三公可謂尊用矣斯知六蓺之歸不務明政以補主上之缺持爵祿之重阿順苟合嚴威酷刑聽高邪說廢適立庶諸侯已畔斯乃欲諫爭不亦末乎人皆以斯極忠而被五刑死察其本乃與俗議之異不然斯之功且與周召列矣

索隱述贊曰

鼠在所居　人固擇地　斯效智力
功立名遂　置酒咸陽　人臣極位
一夫誑惑　變易神器　國喪身誅
本同末異

李斯列傳第二十七　史記八十七

蒙恬列傳第二十八　史記八十八

蒙恬者其先齊人也恬大父蒙驁索隱曰驁音敖又鄒氏音五到反自齊事秦昭王官至上卿秦莊襄王元年蒙驁爲秦將伐韓取城皐滎陽作置三川郡二年蒙驁攻趙取三十七城始皇三年蒙驁攻韓取十三城五年蒙驁攻魏取二十城作置東郡始皇七年蒙驁卒驁子曰武武子曰恬恬嘗書獄典文學索隱曰謂恬嘗學獄法遂作獄官典文學始皇二十三年蒙武爲秦裨將軍與王翦攻楚大破之殺項燕二十四年蒙武攻楚虜楚王蒙恬弟毅始皇二十六

年蒙恬因家世得爲秦將攻齊大破之拜爲內史秦已并天下乃使蒙恬將三十萬衆北逐戎狄收河南正義曰謂靈及勝等州築長城因地形用制險塞起臨洮徐廣曰屬隴西至遼東正義曰遼東郡在遼水東始皇築長城東至遼水西南至海之上延袤萬餘里於是渡河據陽山徐廣曰五原西安陽縣北有陰山陰山在河南陽山在河北逶蛇而北暴師於外十餘年居上郡是時蒙恬威振匈奴始皇甚尊寵蒙氏信任賢之而親近蒙毅位至上卿出則參乘入則御前恬任外事而毅常爲內謀名爲忠信故雖諸將相莫敢與之爭焉趙高者諸趙疏遠屬也趙

高昆弟數人皆生隱宮（徐廣曰爲宦者。索隱曰劉氏云蓋其父犯宮刑妻子沒爲奴婢妻後野合所生子皆承趙姓並宮之故云兄弟生於隱宮也）其母被刑僇世世卑賤秦王聞高彊力通於獄法舉以爲中車府令高即私事公子胡亥喻之決獄高有大罪秦王令蒙毅法治之毅不敢阿法當高罪死除其宦籍帝以高之敦於事也（徐廣曰敦一作敏）赦之復其官爵始皇欲游天下道九原（正義曰九原郡今勝州連谷縣是）直抵甘泉（正義曰宮在雍州）乃使蒙恬通道自九原抵甘泉塹山堙谷千八百里道未就始皇三十七年冬行出游會稽並海上（索隱曰並音白浪反）北走琅邪（索隱曰走音奏走猶向也鄒氏音趨趨亦向義於字則乖）道病使蒙毅還禱山川未反始皇至沙丘崩秘之羣臣莫知是時丞相李斯少子胡亥中車府令趙高常從高雅得幸於胡亥欲立之又怨蒙毅法治之而不爲已也因有賊心乃與丞相李斯公子胡亥陰謀立胡亥爲太子太子已立遣使者以罪賜公子扶蘇蒙恬死扶蘇已死蒙恬疑而復請之使者以蒙恬屬吏更置胡亥以李斯舍人爲護軍使者還報胡亥已聞扶蘇死即欲釋蒙恬趙高恐蒙氏復貴而用事怨之毅還至趙高因爲胡亥忠計欲以滅蒙氏乃言曰臣聞先帝欲舉賢立太子久矣而毅諫曰不可若知賢而愈不立則是不忠而惑主也索隱曰愈一作俞俞即踰也音史謂知太子賢而踰久不立是不忠也以臣愚意不若誅之胡亥聽而繫蒙毅於代正義曰今代州也因禱山川至代而繫之前已因蒙恬於陽周喪至咸陽已葬太子立爲二世皇帝而趙高親近日夜毀惡蒙氏求其罪過舉劾之子嬰進諫曰臣聞故趙王遷殺其良臣李牧而用顏聚燕王喜陰用荆軻之謀而倍秦之約齊王建殺其故世忠臣而用后勝之議此三君者皆各以變古者失其國而殃及其

身今蒙氏秦之大臣謀士也而主欲一旦棄去之臣竊以爲不可臣聞輕慮者不可以治國獨智者不可以存君徐廣曰一無此字誅殺忠臣而立無節行之人是內使羣臣不相信而外使鬬士之意離也臣竊以爲不可胡亥不聽而遣御史曲宮乘傳之代索隱曰曲姓宮名令蒙毅曰先主欲立太子而卿難之今丞相以卿爲不忠罪及其宗朕不忍乃賜卿死亦甚幸矣卿其圖之毅對曰以臣不能得先主之意則臣少宧順幸沒世可謂知意矣索隱曰蒙毅言已少事始皇順旨蒙恩幸至始皇沒世可謂知上意也以臣不知太

子之能則太子獨從周旋天下去諸公子絶遠臣無所疑矣夫先主之舉用太子數年之積也臣乃何言之敢諫何慮之敢謀非敢飾辭以避死也爲羞累先主之名願大夫爲慮焉使臣得死情實且夫順成全者道之所貴也刑殺者道之所卒也昔者秦穆公殺三良而死罪百里奚而非其罪也故立號曰繆昭襄王殺武安君白起楚平王殺伍奢吳王夫差殺伍子胥此四君者皆爲大失而天下非之以其君爲不明以是籍於諸侯索隱曰言其惡聲狼籍布於諸國劉氏云諸侯皆記其惡於史籍非也故曰用

道治者不殺無罪而罰不加於無辜唯大夫留心使者知胡亥之意不聽蒙毅之言殺之二世又遣使者之陽周令蒙恬曰君之過多矣而卿弟毅有大罪法及內史恬曰自吾先人及至子孫積功信於秦三世矣今臣將兵三十餘萬身雖因繫其勢足以倍畔自知必死而守義者不敢辱先人之教以不忘先主也昔周成王初立未離襁緥周公旦負王以朝卒定天下及成王有病甚殆公旦自揃其爪以沈於河曰王未有識是旦執事有罪殃旦受其不祥乃書而藏之

記府可謂信矣及王能治國有賊臣言周公旦欲爲亂久矣王若不備必有大事王乃大怒周公旦走而奔於楚成王觀於記府得周公旦沈書乃流涕曰孰謂周公旦欲爲亂乎殺言之者而反周公旦故周書曰必參而伍之索隱曰參謂三卿五即五大夫欲參伍更議今恬之宗世無二心而事卒如此是必孽臣逆亂徐廣曰一作辭内陵之道也夫成王失而復振則卒昌桀殺關龍逢紂殺王子比干而不悔身死則國亡臣故曰過可振而諫可覺也索隱曰此故曰者必先志有此言蒙恬引之以成説也今不知出何書耳振者救也然語亦倒以言前人受諫可覺則其過乃可救也察

於參伍上聖之法也凡臣之言非以求免於咎也將以諫而死願陛下爲萬民思從道也使者曰臣受詔行法於將軍不敢以將軍言聞於上也蒙恬喟然太息曰我何罪於天無過而死乎良久徐曰恬罪固當死矣起臨洮屬之遼東城壍萬餘里此其中不能無絶地脈哉此乃恬之罪也乃吞藥自殺

太史公曰吾適北邊自直道歸行觀蒙恬所爲秦築長城亭障壍山堙谷通直道固輕百姓力矣夫秦之初滅諸侯天下之心未定痍傷者未

瘳而恬爲名將不以此時彊諫振百姓之急養老存孤務修衆庶之和而阿意興功此其兄弟遇誅不亦宜乎何乃罪地脈哉

索隱述贊曰

蒙氏秦將　內史忠賢　長城首築

萬里安邊　趙高矯制　扶蘇死焉

絕地何罪　勞人是愆　呼天欲訴

三代良然

蒙恬列傳第二十八　史記八十八

張耳陳餘列傳第二十九　史記八十九

索隱曰張耳吳芮勢侔楚漢位埒齊韓俱懷從沛之心咸享誓河之業爵在列侯之上家傳累代之基長沙既曰令終趙王亦謂善始並可列同世家焉

張耳者大梁人也索隱曰呂瓚云今陳留大梁城是也其少時及魏公子毋忌爲客張耳嘗亡命游外黃索隱曰晉灼曰命者名也謂脫名籍而逃崔浩曰亡無也命名也逃匿則削除名籍故以逃爲亡命地理志外黃屬陳留外黃富人女甚美嫁庸奴亡其夫徐廣曰一云其夫亡也去抵父客如淳曰父時故賓客○索隱曰如淳曰抵歸也音丁禮反父客素知張耳乃謂女曰必欲求賢夫從張耳女聽乃卒爲請決嫁之張耳索隱曰謂女請父客爲決絕其夫而嫁之張耳張耳是時脫身游女家厚奉給張耳張耳以故致千里客乃宦魏爲外黃令名由此益賢

陳餘者亦大梁人也好儒術數游趙苦陘張晏曰苦陘漢章帝改曰漢昌○索隱曰地理志屬中山○正義曰音邢邢州唐昌縣富人公乘氏以其女妻之亦知陳餘非庸人也餘年少父事張耳兩人相與爲刎頸交索隱曰崔浩云言要齊生死斷頸無悔秦之滅大梁也張耳家外黃高祖爲布衣時嘗數從張耳游客數月秦滅魏數歲已聞此兩人魏之名士也購求有得張耳千金陳餘五百金張耳陳餘乃變名姓俱之陳爲里監門張晏曰監門里正衞也以自

食兩人相對里吏嘗有過笞陳餘陳餘欲起張耳躡之（徐廣曰一作攝）使受笞吏去張耳乃引陳餘之桑下而數之曰始吾與公言何如今見小辱而欲死一吏乎陳餘然之秦詔書購求兩人兩人亦反用門者以令里中（索隱曰案門者即餘耳也自以其名而號令里中詐更別求也）陳涉起蘄至入陳兵數萬張耳陳餘上謁陳涉涉及左右生平數聞張耳陳餘賢未嘗見見即大喜陳中豪傑父老乃說陳涉曰將軍身被堅執銳率士卒以誅暴秦復立楚社稷存亡繼絕功德宜爲王且夫監臨天下諸將不爲王不

可願將軍立爲楚王也陳涉問此兩人兩人對曰夫秦爲無道破人國家滅人社稷絕人後世罷百姓之力盡百姓之財將軍瞋目張膽出萬死不顧一生之計爲天下除殘也今始至陳而王之示天下私願將軍毋王急引兵而西遣人立六國後自爲樹黨爲秦益敵也敵多則力分與衆則兵彊如此野無交兵縣無守城誅暴秦據咸陽以令諸侯諸侯亡而得立以德服之如此則帝業成矣今獨王陳恐天下解也（正義曰解紀賣反言天下諸侯見陳勝稱王王陳皆懈墮不相從也）陳涉不聽遂立爲王陳餘乃

復說陳王曰大王舉梁楚而西務在入關未及收河北也臣嘗游趙知其豪桀及地形願請奇兵北略趙地於是陳王以故所善陳人武臣爲將軍邵騷爲護軍以張耳陳餘爲左右校尉予卒三千人北略趙地武臣等從白馬渡河索隱曰案鄧展酈食其云白馬之津則白馬津是渡處其地與黎陽對岸至諸縣說其豪桀曰曰至河北縣說之秦爲亂政虐刑以殘賊天下數十年矣北有長城之域南有五嶺之戍漢書音義曰嶺有五因以爲名在交阯界中也○索隱曰裴氏廣州記云大庾始安臨賀桂陽揭陽斯五嶺外內騷動百姓罷敝頭會箕斂漢書音義曰家家人頭數出穀以箕斂之以供軍費財匱

力盡民不聊生重之以苛法峻刑使天下父子不相安陳王奮臂爲天下倡始王楚之地方二千里莫不響應家自爲怒人自爲鬬各報其怨而攻其讎縣殺其令丞郡殺其守尉今已張大楚王陳使吳廣周文將卒百萬西擊秦於此時而不成封侯之業者非人豪也諸君試相與計之夫天下同心而苦秦久矣因天下之力而攻無道之君報父兄之怨而成割地有土之業此士之一時也豪桀皆然其言乃行收兵得數萬人號武臣爲武信君下趙十城餘皆城守莫肯

下乃引兵東北擊范陽范陽人蒯通說范陽令曰（漢書曰范陽令徐公）竊聞公之將死故弔雖然賀公得通而生范陽令曰何以弔之對曰秦法重足下為范陽令十年矣殺人之父孤人之子斷人之足黥人之首不可勝數然而慈父孝子莫敢傳刃（徐廣曰傳音㦸）公之腹中者（李奇曰東方人以物揷地皆為傳）畏秦法耳今天下大亂秦法不施然則慈父孝子且傳刃公之腹中以成其名此臣之所以弔公也今諸侯畔秦矣武信君兵且至而君堅守范陽少年皆爭殺君下武信君君急遣臣見武信君可轉禍

為福在今矣范陽令乃使蒯通見武信君曰足下必將戰勝然後略地攻得然後下城臣竊以為過矣誠聽臣之計可不攻而降城不戰而略地傳檄而千里定可乎武信君曰何謂也蒯通曰今范陽令宜整頓其士卒以守戰者也怯而畏死貪而重富貴故欲先天下降畏君以為秦所置吏誅殺如前十城也然今范陽少年亦方殺其令自以城距君君何不齎臣侯印拜范陽令范陽令則以城下君少年亦不敢殺其令令范陽令乘朱輪華轂使驅馳燕趙郊燕趙郊見

之皆曰此范陽令先下者也即喜矣燕趙城可毋戰而降也此臣之所謂傳檄而千里定者也武信君從其計因使蒯通賜范陽令侯印趙地聞之不戰以城下者三十餘城至邯鄲張耳陳餘聞周章軍入關至戲却蘇林曰戲地名却兵退也○正義曰戲音羲出驪山又聞諸將爲陳王徇地多以讒毀得罪誅怨陳王不用其筴不以爲將而以爲校尉乃說武臣曰陳王起蘄至陳而王非必立六國後將軍今以三千人下趙數十城獨介居河北晉灼曰介音夏瓚曰方言云介特也不王無以填之且陳王聽讒還報恐不脫

於禍又不如立其兄弟不即立趙後將軍毋失時時間不容息索隱曰以言舉事不可失時時機之迅速其間不容一喘息須也武臣乃聽之遂立爲趙王以陳餘爲大將軍張耳爲右丞相邵騷爲左丞相使人報陳王陳王大怒欲盡族武臣等家而發兵擊趙陳王相國房君諫曰秦未亡而誅武臣等家此又生一秦也不如因而賀之使急引兵西擊秦陳王然之從其計徙繫武臣等家宮中封張耳子敖爲成都君陳王使使者賀趙令趣發兵西入關張耳陳餘說武臣曰王王趙非楚意特以計賀王楚已

滅秦必加兵於趙願王毋西兵北徇燕代南收河內以自廣趙南據大河北有燕代楚雖勝秦必不敢制趙趙王以為然因不西兵而使韓廣略燕李良略常山張黶略上黨韓廣至燕燕人因立廣為燕王（徐廣曰九月也）趙王乃與張耳陳餘北略地燕界趙王閒出為燕軍所得燕將囚之欲與分趙地半乃歸王使者往燕燕輒殺之以求地張耳陳餘患之有廝養卒謝其舍中曰（如淳曰廝賤者也公羊傳曰廝役扈養韋昭曰析薪為廝炊烹為養晉灼曰以辭相告曰謝也○索隱曰謂其同舍中之人也漢書作舍人）吾為公說燕與趙王載歸舍中皆笑曰使者往

十餘輩輒死若何以能得王乃走燕壁燕將見之問燕將曰知臣何欲燕將曰若欲得趙王耳曰君知張耳陳餘何如人也燕將曰賢人也曰知其志何欲曰欲得其王耳趙養卒乃笑曰君未知此兩人所欲也夫武臣張耳陳餘杖馬箠下趙數十城（張晏曰言其不用兵革驅策而已也○索隱曰杖音丈箠音之委反）此亦各欲南面而王豈欲為卿相終已邪夫臣與主豈可同日而道哉顧其勢初定未敢參分而王且以少長先立武臣為王以持趙心今趙地已服此兩人亦欲分趙而王時未可耳今君乃囚

趙王此兩人名爲求趙王實欲燕殺之此兩人分趙自立夫以一趙尚易燕況以兩賢王左提右挈而責殺王之罪（徐廣曰平原君傳曰事成執右券以責也券契義同耳）滅燕易矣燕將以爲然乃歸趙王養卒爲御而歸

李良已定常山還報趙王復使良略太原至石邑（索隱曰地理志屬常山）秦兵塞井陘未能前秦將詐稱二世使人遺李良書不封（張晏曰欲其漏泄君臣相疑）曰良嘗事我得顯幸良誠能反趙爲秦赦良罪貴良良得書疑不信乃還之邯鄲益請兵未至道逢趙王姊出飲從百餘騎李良望見以爲王伏謁道

旁王姊醉不知其將使騎謝李良李良素貴起慙其從官有一人曰天下畔秦能者先立且趙王素出將軍下今女兒乃不爲將軍下車請追殺之李良已得秦書固欲反趙未決因此怒遣人追殺王姊道中乃遂將其兵襲邯鄲邯鄲不知竟殺武臣邵騷趙人多爲張耳陳餘耳目者以故得脫出收其兵得數萬人客有說張耳曰兩君羈旅而欲附趙難獨立立趙後扶以義可就功（索隱曰案羈旅勢弱難以立功也獨有立六國趙王之後可以成功）乃求得趙歇（徐廣曰正月也音烏鍇反　駰案張晏曰趙之苗裔）立爲趙王居信都（徐廣

曰後項羽改曰襄国李良進兵擊陳餘陳餘敗李良李良走歸章邯章邯引兵至邯鄲皆徙其民河內夷其城郭張耳與趙王歇走入鉅鹿城王離圍之陳餘北收常山兵得數萬人軍鉅鹿北章邯軍鉅鹿南棘原築甬道屬河餉王離王離兵食多急攻鉅鹿鉅鹿城中食盡兵少張耳數使人召前陳餘陳餘自度兵少不敵秦不敢前數月張耳大怒怨陳餘使張黶陳澤正義音釋往讓陳餘曰始吾與公為刎頸交今王與耳旦暮且死而公擁兵數萬不肯相救安在其相為死苟必信胡

不赴秦軍俱死且有十一二相全正義曰十中冀一兩勝秦陳餘曰吾度前終不能救趙徒盡亡軍且餘所以不俱死欲為趙王張君報秦今必俱死如以肉委餓虎何益張黶陳澤曰事已急要以俱死立信安知後慮陳餘曰吾死顧以為無益必如公言乃使五千人令張黶陳澤先嘗秦軍索隱曰崔浩云嘗猶試至皆沒當是時燕齊楚聞趙急皆來救張敖亦北收代兵得萬餘人來皆壁餘旁未敢擊秦項羽兵數絕章邯甬道王離軍乏食項羽悉引兵渡河遂破章邯徐廣曰三年十二月也章邯引兵解諸侯軍

乃敢擊圍鉅鹿秦軍遂虜王離涉閒自殺卒存鉅鹿者楚力也於是趙王歇張耳乃得出鉅鹿謝諸侯張耳與陳餘相見責讓陳餘以不肯救趙及問張黶陳澤所在陳餘怒曰張黶陳澤以必死責臣臣使將五千人先嘗秦軍皆沒不出張耳不信以為殺之數問陳餘陳餘怒曰不意君之望臣深也索隱曰望怨責也豈以臣為重去將哉索隱曰案重訓難也或云重惜也乃脫解印綬推予張耳張耳亦愕不受陳餘起如廁客有說張耳曰臣聞天與不取反受其咎索隱曰此辭出國語今陳將軍與君印君

不受反天不祥急取之張耳乃佩其印收其麾下而陳餘還亦望張耳不讓正義曰言陳餘如廁還亦怨望張耳不讓其印遂趨出張耳遂收其兵陳餘獨與麾下所善數百人之河上澤中漁獵由此陳餘張耳遂有郤趙王歇復居信都張耳從項羽諸侯入關漢元年二月項羽立諸侯王張耳雅游韋昭曰雅素也○索隱曰鄭氏云雅故也韋昭云雅素然素亦故也雅游言慣游從故多為人所稱譽人多為之言項羽亦素數聞張耳賢乃分趙立張耳為常山王治信都信都更名襄國陳餘客多說項羽曰陳餘張耳一體有功於趙項羽以陳餘不從入關聞

其在南皮（索隱曰地理志屬勃海○正義曰故城在滄州南皮縣北四里也）即以南皮旁三縣以封之而徙趙王歇王代（徐廣曰都代縣）張耳之國陳餘愈益怒曰張耳與餘功等也今張耳王餘獨侯此項羽不平及齊王田榮畔楚陳餘乃使夏說說田榮曰（正義曰上說音悅下式銳反）項羽為天下宰不平盡王諸將善地徙故王王惡地今趙王乃居代願王假臣兵請以南皮為扞蔽田榮欲樹黨於趙以反楚乃遣兵從陳餘陳餘因悉三縣兵襲常山王張耳張耳敗走念諸侯無可歸者曰漢王與我有舊故（張晏曰漢王為布衣時嘗從張耳游）而項羽

又彊立我我欲之楚（張晏曰羽既彊盛又為所立且是以狐疑莫知所往也）甘公曰（文穎曰善說星者甘氏也○索隱曰天官書云齊甘公藝文志云楚有甘公齊楚不同未知孰是劉歆七略云公一名德）漢王之入關五星聚東井東井者秦分也先至必霸楚雖彊後必屬漢故耳走漢（徐廣曰二年十月也）漢王亦還定三秦方圍章邯廢丘張耳謁漢王漢王厚遇之陳餘已敗張耳皆復收趙地迎趙王於代復為趙王趙王德陳餘立以為代王陳餘為趙王弱國初定不之國留傅趙王而使夏說以相國守代漢二年東擊楚使使告趙欲與俱陳餘曰漢殺張耳乃從於是漢王求人類張耳

者斬之持其頭遺陳餘陳餘乃遣兵助漢漢之敗於彭城西陳餘亦復覺張耳不死即背漢漢三年韓信已定魏地遣張耳與韓信擊破趙井陘徐廣曰三年十月斬陳餘泜水上徐廣曰在常山音遲一音丁禮反○索隱曰蘇林音祗晉灼音邸今俗呼此水則然案地理志音脂則蘇音爲得郭景純注山海經云泜水出常山中丘縣○正義曰在趙州贊皇縣界追殺趙王歇襄國漢立張耳爲趙王徐廣曰四年十一月駰案漢書四年夏漢五年張耳薨謚爲景王子敖嗣立爲趙王高祖長女魯元公主爲趙王敖后漢七年高祖從平城過趙趙王朝夕袒韝蔽徐廣曰韝者臂捍也自上食禮甚卑有子壻禮高祖箕倨詈

甚慢易之索隱曰崔浩云屈膝坐其形如箕趙相貫高趙午等年六十餘徐廣曰田叔傳云趙相趙午等數十人皆怒然則或宜言六十餘人故張耳客也生平爲氣乃怒曰吾王孱王也孟康曰音如孱潺之孱冀州人謂懦弱爲孱韋昭曰仁謹貌○索隱曰案服虔音鉏閑反弱小貌也小顏音仕連反說王曰夫天下豪桀並起能者先立今王事高祖甚恭而高祖無禮請爲王殺之張敖齧其指出血索隱曰案小顏云齧指以表至誠爲其約誓曰君何言之誤且先人亡國賴高祖得復國德流子孫秋豪皆高祖力也願君無復出口貫高趙午等十餘人皆相謂曰乃吾等非也吾王長者不倍德且吾等義不辱今怨高祖辱

我王故欲殺之何乃汚王爲乎索隱曰漢書作汙蕭該音一故反說文云汙薉也令事成歸王事敗獨身坐耳漢八年上從東垣還過趙貫高等乃壁人柏人索隱曰謂於柏人縣館舍壁中著人欲爲變也。正義曰柏人故城在邢州柏人縣西北十二里即高祖宿處也要之置韋昭曰爲供置也。索隱曰文穎云置人廁壁中以伺高祖也張晏云鑿壁空之令人止中也今按云置廁者置人於複壁中謂之置廁則者隱側之處因以爲言也亦音惻上過欲宿心動問曰縣名爲何曰柏人柏人者迫於人也不宿而去漢九年貫高怨家知其謀乃上變告之於是上皆并逮捕趙王貫高等十餘人皆爭自剄貫高獨怒罵曰誰令公爲之今王實無謀而并捕王公等皆死

誰白王不反者乃轞車膠致正義曰謂其車上著板四周如檻形膠密不得開送致京師也與王詣長安治張敖之罪上乃詔趙羣臣賓客有敢從王皆族貫高與客孟舒等十餘人皆自髡鉗爲王家奴從來貫高至對獄曰獨吾屬爲之王實不知吏治榜笞數千刺剟徐廣曰丁劣反。索隱曰案剟亦刺也漢書作刺爇張晏云爇灼也說文云燒也應劭云以鐵刺之身無可擊者終不復言呂后數言張王以魯元公主故不宜有此上怒曰使張敖據天下豈少而女乎不聽廷尉以貫高事辭聞上曰壯士誰知者以私問之贊曰以私情相問中大夫泄公曰正義曰泄姓也史有泄私臣之

邑子素知之此固趙國立名義不侵爲然諾者
也上使泄公持節問之箯輿前徐廣曰箯音鞭駰案韋昭曰輿如今
輿牀人輿以行○索隱曰服虔云音編編竹木如今峻可以輿也何休注公羊筍音峻筍者竹箯一名編齊魯已北名
爲筍郭璞三蒼注云箯輿罊土器仰視曰泄公邪泄公勞苦如生平
驩與語問張王果有計謀不高曰人情寧不各
愛其父母妻子乎今吾三族皆以論死豈以王
易吾親哉顧爲王實不反獨吾等爲之具道本
指所以爲者王不知狀於是泄公入具以報上
乃赦趙王上賢貫高爲人能立然諾使泄公具
告之曰張王已出因赦貫高貫高喜曰吾王審

出乎泄公曰然泄公曰上多足下故赦足下貫
高曰所以不死一身無餘者白張王不反也今
王已出吾責已塞死不恨矣且人臣有簒殺之
名何面目復事上哉縱上不殺我我不愧於心
乎乃仰絶肮遂死韋昭曰肮咽也○索隱曰蘇林云肮頸大脉也俗所謂胡脉音下郎反蕭
該或音下浪反當此之時名聞天下張敖已出以尚魯
元故封爲宣平侯索隱曰韋昭曰尚奉也不敢言取崔浩云奉事公主小顏云尚配也易得
尚于中行王弼亦以尚爲配恐非其義於是上賢張王諸客以鉗奴從
張王入關無不爲諸侯相郡守者及孝惠高后
文帝孝景時張王客子孫皆得爲二千石張敖

高后六年薨關中記曰張敖冢在安陵東。正義曰魯元公主墓在咸陽縣西北二十五里次東有張敖冢與公主同域又張耳墓在咸陽縣東三十三里子偃爲魯元王以母呂后女故呂后封爲魯元王索隱曰案謂偃以其母號而封也元王弱兄弟少乃封張敖他姬子二人壽爲樂昌侯徐廣曰漢紀張酺傳曰張敖之子壽封樂昌侯食細陽之池陽鄉也侈爲信都侯高后崩諸呂無道大臣誅之而廢魯元王及樂昌侯信都侯孝文帝即位復封故魯元王偃爲南宮侯續張氏張敖謚武侯張偃之孫有罪絕信都侯名侈樂昌侯名壽

太史公曰張耳陳餘世傳所稱賢者其賓客廝役莫非天下俊桀所居國無不取卿相者然張耳陳餘始居約時漢書音義曰在貧賤時也相然信以死豈顧問哉索隱曰葛洪要用字苑云然猶爾也謂相和同諸者何也謂然諾相信雖死不顧也及據國爭權卒相滅亡何鄉者相慕用之誠後相倍之戾也豈非以利哉索隱曰有本作私利交漢書作勢利交故廉頗傳云天下以市道交君有勢則從君無勢則去此固其理也名譽雖高賓客雖盛所由殆與太伯延陵季子異矣

索隱述贊曰

張耳陳餘　天下豪俊　忘年羈旅　刎頸相信

耳圍鉅鹿　餘兵不進　張既望深　陳乃去印

勢利傾奪　隙末成釁

張耳陳餘列傳第二十九　史記八十九

魏豹彭越列傳第三十　史記九十

魏豹者故魏諸公子也其兄魏咎故魏時封爲甯陵君索隱曰案彭越傳云魏豹魏王咎從弟眞魏後也晉灼云甯陵梁國縣也即今寧陵是秦滅魏遷咎爲家人陳勝之起王也正義王于放反咎往從之陳王使魏人周市徇魏地魏地已下欲相與立周市爲魏王周市曰天下昏亂忠臣乃見索隱曰老子曰國家昏亂有忠臣此取以爲說也今天下共畔秦其義必立魏王後乃可齊趙使車各五十乘立周市爲魏王市辭不受迎魏咎於陳五反陳王乃遣立咎爲魏王徐廣曰元年十二月也章邯已破陳王乃進兵擊魏

王於臨濟正義曰故城在淄州高苑縣北二里本漢縣魏王乃使周市出請救於齊楚齊楚遣項它田巴將兵隨市救魏索隱曰案項它楚將田巴齊將也○正義它徒多反章邯遂擊破殺周市等軍圍臨濟咎爲其民約降約定咎自燒殺魏豹亡走楚徐廣曰二年六月楚懷王予魏豹數千人復徇魏地項羽已破秦降章邯豹下魏二十餘城立豹爲魏王豹引精兵從項羽入關漢元年項羽封諸侯欲有梁地乃徙魏王豹於河東都平陽正義曰今晉州爲西魏王漢王還定三秦渡臨晉正義曰臨晉在同州朝邑縣界魏王豹以國屬焉遂從擊楚於彭城漢

敗還至滎陽豹請歸視親病至國即絕河津畔漢漢王聞魏豹反方東憂楚未及擊謂酈生曰緩頰往說魏豹能下之吾以萬戶封若酈生說豹豹謝曰人生一世閒如白駒過隙耳索隱曰莊子云無異騏驥之馳過隙則謂馬也小顏云白駒謂日影也隙壁隙也以言速疾若日影過壁隙也今漢王慢而侮人罵詈諸侯羣臣如罵奴耳非有上下禮節也吾不忍復見也於是漢王遣韓信擊虜豹於河東徐廣曰二年九月也傳詣滎陽以豹國為郡高祖本紀曰置三郡河東太原上黨漢王令豹守滎陽楚圍之急周苛遂殺魏豹

彭越者昌邑人也正義曰漢武更山陽為昌國有梁丘鄉梁丘故城在曹州城武縣東北三十三里字仲常漁鉅野澤中為羣盜陳勝項梁之起少年或謂越曰諸豪桀相立畔秦仲可以來亦效之彭越曰兩龍方鬬且待之居歲餘澤閒少年相聚百餘人往從彭越曰請仲為長越謝曰臣不願與諸君少年彊請乃許與期旦日日出會後期者斬索隱曰旦日謂明日之朝日出時也旦日日出十餘人後後者至日中於是越謝曰臣老諸君彊以為長今期而多後不可盡誅誅最後者一人令校長斬之皆笑曰何至是請後不敢於是越乃

引一人斬之設壇祭乃令徒屬徒屬皆大驚畏越莫敢仰視乃行略地收諸侯散卒得千餘人沛公之從碭北（正義曰音唐朗反宋州碭山縣）擊昌邑彭越助之昌邑未下沛公引兵西彭越亦將其衆居鉅野中收魏散卒項籍入關王諸侯還歸彭越衆萬餘人毋所屬漢元年秋齊王田榮畔項王漢乃使人賜彭越將軍印使下濟陰以擊楚楚命蕭公角（正義曰蕭縣令楚縣令稱公角名）將兵擊越越大破楚軍漢王二年春與魏王豹及諸侯東擊楚彭越將其兵三萬餘人歸漢於外黃漢王曰彭將軍收魏

地得十餘城欲急立魏後今西魏王豹亦魏王咎從弟也眞魏後乃拜彭越爲魏相國擅將其兵略定梁地（索隱曰擅猶專也）漢王之敗彭城解而西也彭越皆復亡其所下城獨將其兵北居河上（正義曰滑州河上）漢王三年彭越常往來爲漢游兵擊楚絕其後糧於梁地漢四年冬項王與漢王相距滎陽彭越攻下睢陽外黃十七城（正義曰睢陽宋州宋城也外黃在汴州雍丘縣東）項王聞之乃使曹咎守城皋（正義曰河南府汜水是）自東收彭越所下城邑皆復爲楚（正義曰爲于僞反）越將其兵北走穀城（正義曰在濟州東阿縣東二十六里是）漢五年秋項

王之南走陽夏【正義曰夏古雅反陳州太康縣也】彭越復下昌邑旁二十餘城得穀十餘萬斛以給漢王食漢王敗使使召彭越并力擊楚越曰魏地初定尚畏楚未可去漢王追楚為項籍所敗固陵【正義曰固陵名在陳州宛丘縣西北三十二里】乃謂留侯曰諸侯兵不從為之奈何留侯曰齊王信之立非君王之意信亦不自堅彭越本定梁地功多始君王以魏豹故拜彭越為魏相國今豹死毋後且越亦欲王而君王不蚤定與此兩國約即勝楚睢陽以北至穀城【正義曰從宋州已北至鄆州以西曹濮沐滑並與彭越】皆以王彭相國從陳以東

傅【音附】海【正義曰從陳潁州北以東亳四徐淮北之地東至海并淮南淮陰之邑盡與韓信韓信又先有故齊舊地】與齊王信齊王信家在楚此其意欲復得故邑君王能出捐此地許二人二人今可致即不能事未可知也於是漢王乃發使使彭越如留侯策使者至彭越乃悉引兵會垓下【正義曰在亳州也】遂破楚五年項籍已死春立彭越為梁王都定陶【正義曰曹州】六年朝陳九年十年皆來朝長安十年秋陳豨反代地高帝自往擊至邯鄲徵兵梁王梁王稱病使將將兵詣邯鄲高帝怒使人讓梁王梁王恐欲自往謝其將扈輒曰王始不往見讓

而往往則爲禽矣不如遂發兵反梁王不聽稱病梁王怒其太僕欲斬之太僕亡走漢告梁王與扈輒謀反於是上使使掩梁王梁王不覺捕梁王囚之雒陽有司治反形已具張晏曰扈輒勸越反越不聽而云反形已具有司非也瓚曰扈輒勸越反而越不誅輒是反形已具請論如法上赦以爲庶人傳處蜀青衣文穎曰青衣縣名在蜀瓚曰今漢嘉是也○索隱曰蘇林云縣名今爲臨邛瓚說爲是西至鄭索隱曰地理志鄭屬京兆○正義曰華州逢呂后從長安來欲之雒陽道見彭王彭王爲呂后泣涕自言無罪願處故昌邑呂后許諾與俱東至雒陽呂后白上曰彭王壯士今徙之蜀此自遺患正義曰上唯季反不如遂誅之妾謹與俱來於是呂后乃令其舍人告彭越復謀反廷尉王恬開奏請族之上乃可遂夷越宗族國除

太史公曰魏豹彭越雖故賤然已席卷千里正義曰言魏地闊千里如席卷舒南面稱孤喋血乘勝日有聞矣徐廣曰一作啑韓傳亦有喋血語也○索隱曰音牒喋猶蹀也殺敵蹀血而行孝文紀喋血京師是也懷畔逆之意及敗不死而虜囚身被刑戮何哉中材已上且羞其行況王者乎彼無異故智略絕人獨患無身耳得攝尺寸之柄其雲蒸龍變欲有所會其度以故幽囚而不辭云

索隱述贊曰

魏咎兄弟　因時而王　豹後屬楚

其國遂亡　仲起昌邑　歸漢外黄

往來聲援　再續軍糧　徵兵不往

葅醢何傷

魏豹彭越列傳第三十　史記九十

黥布列傳第三十一

黥布者六人也姓英氏索隱曰地理志盧江有六縣蘇林曰今爲六安也布本姓英英國名也咎繇之後布以少時有人相云當刑而王故漢雜事云布改姓黥以厭當之也○正義曰故六城在壽州安豐縣西南百三十三里按黥布封淮南王都六即此城又春秋傳六與蓼咎繇之後或封於英六蓋英後改爲蓼也秦時爲布衣少年有客相之曰當刑而王及壯坐法黥布欣然笑曰人相我當刑而王幾是乎徐廣曰幾一作豈駰謂幾近也○索隱曰臣瓚音機楚漢春秋作豈是乎故徐廣云一作豈劉氏音祈祈者語辭也義亦通人有聞者共俳笑之索隱曰謂衆共以俳優輩笑之布已論輸麗山正義曰言布論決受黥竟見麗山作陵也時會稽郡輸身徒麗山之徒數十萬人布皆與其徒長豪桀交通迺率其曹偶亡之江

中爲羣盜索隱曰曹輩也偶類也謂徒之輩類陳勝之起也布迺見番君與其衆叛秦聚兵數千人番君以其女妻之章邯之滅陳勝破呂臣軍布乃引兵北擊秦左右校破之清波引兵而東聞項梁定江東會稽正義曰時會稽郡所理在吳闔閭城中涉江而西陳嬰以項氏世爲楚將迺以兵屬項梁渡淮南英布蒲將軍亦以兵屬項梁項梁涉淮而西擊景駒秦嘉等布常冠軍項梁至薛正義曰薛古城在徐州滕縣界也聞陳王定死迺立楚懷王項梁號爲武信君英布爲當陽君正義曰南郡當陽縣也項梁敗死定陶懷王徙都彭城諸將英

布亦皆保聚彭城當是時秦急圍趙趙數使人請救懷王使宋義爲上將范曾爲末將項籍爲次將英布蒲將軍皆爲將軍悉屬宋義北救趙及項籍殺宋義於河上懷王因立籍爲上將軍諸將皆屬項籍項籍使布先涉渡河擊秦布數有利籍迺悉引兵涉河從之遂破秦軍降章邯等楚兵常勝功冠諸侯諸侯兵皆以服屬楚者以布數以少敗衆也項籍之引兵西至新安正義曰新安故城在河南府澠池縣東二十二里又使布等夜擊坑章邯秦卒二十餘萬人至關不得入又使布等先從閒道

破關下軍索隱曰鄒氏云閒音閑閑謂私也今以閒音紀莧反閒道即他道也猶若反閒之義遂得入至咸陽布常爲軍鋒索隱曰案漢書作楚軍前簿簿者鹵簿項王封諸將立布爲九江王都六漢元年四月諸侯皆罷戲下各就國項氏立懷王爲義帝徙都長沙迺陰令九江王布等行擊之其八月布使將擊義帝追殺之郴縣正義曰上丑林反今郴州有義帝冢及祠漢二年齊王田榮畔楚項王往擊齊徵兵九江九江王布稱病不往遣將將數千人行漢之敗楚彭城布又稱病不佐楚項王由此怨布數使使者誚讓漢書音義曰誚責也召布布愈恐不敢往項王方北

夏齊趙西患漢所與者獨九江王又多布材欲親用之以故未擊漢三年漢王擊楚大戰彭城不利出梁地至虞（正義曰今宋州虞城也）謂左右曰（索隱曰案謂隨何）如彼等者無足與計天下事謁者隨何進曰不審陛下所謂漢王曰孰能爲我使淮南令之發兵倍楚留項王於齊數月我之取天下可以百全隨何曰臣請使之廼與二十人俱使淮南至因太宰主之（漢書音義曰淮南太宰作內主也韋昭曰主舍也○索隱曰太宰掌膳食之官）三日不得見隨何因說太宰曰王之不見何必以楚爲彊以漢爲弱此臣之所以爲使使何得見

言之而是邪是大王所欲聞也言之而非邪使何等二十人伏斧質淮南市以明王倍漢而與楚也太宰廼言之王王見之隨何曰漢王使臣敬進書大王御者竊怪大王與楚何親也淮南王曰寡人北鄉而臣事之隨何曰大王與項王俱列爲諸侯北鄉而臣事之必以楚爲彊可以託國也項王伐齊身負板築（李奇曰板牆板也築杵也）以爲士卒先大王宜悉淮南之衆身自將之爲楚軍前鋒今廼發四千人以助楚夫北面而臣事人者固若是乎夫漢王戰於彭城項王未出齊也大

王宜騷（音掃）淮南之兵渡淮日夜會戰彭城下大王撫萬人之衆無一人渡淮者垂拱而觀其孰勝夫託國於人者固若是乎大王提空名以鄉楚而欲厚自託臣竊爲大王不取也然而大王不背楚者以漢爲弱也夫楚兵雖彊天下負之以不義之名（索隱曰負猶被也以不義被其身）以其背盟約而殺義帝也然而楚王恃戰勝自彊漢王收諸侯還守成皐滎陽下蜀漢之粟深溝壁壘分卒守徼乘塞（索隱曰徼謂邊境亭鄣以徼繞邊陲常守之也乘者登也登塞垣而守之）楚人還兵間以梁地深入敵國八九百里（張晏曰羽從齊還當經梁地八九百里迺得羽地○索隱曰案服虔曰梁在楚漢之中央）欲戰則不得攻城則力不能老

弱轉糧千里之外楚兵至滎陽成皐漢堅守而不動進則不得攻退則不能解故曰楚兵不足恃也（徐廣曰恃一作罷言其已困不足復恃也索隱曰案漢書作罷罷音皮）使楚勝漢則諸侯自危懼而相救夫楚之彊適足以致天下之兵耳故楚不如漢其勢易見也今大王不與萬全之漢而自託於危亡之楚臣竊爲大王惑之臣非以淮南之兵足以亡楚也夫大王發兵而倍楚項王必留留數月漢之取天下可以萬全臣請與大王提劍而歸漢漢王必裂地而封

大王又況淮南淮南必大王有也故漢王敬使使臣進愚計願大王之留意也淮南王曰請奉命陰許畔楚與漢未敢泄也楚使者在（文穎曰在淮南王所）方急責英布發兵舍傳舍隨何直入坐楚使者上坐曰九江王已歸漢楚何以得發兵布愕然楚使者起何因說布曰事已搆（索隱曰搆成也）可遂殺楚使者無使歸而疾走漢并力（索隱曰走音奏向也）布曰如使者教因起兵而擊之耳於是殺使者因起兵而攻楚楚使項聲龍且攻淮南項王留而攻下邑（正義曰宋州碭山縣）數月龍且擊淮南破布軍布欲引兵

走漢恐楚王殺之故間行與何俱歸漢淮南王至（徐廣曰三年十二月）上方踞牀洗召布入見布甚大怒悔來欲自殺出就舍帳御飲食從官如漢王居布又大喜過望（正義曰高祖以布先分為王恐其自尊大故峻禮令布折服已而美其帷帳厚其飲食多其從官以悅其心權道也）於是迺使人入九江楚已使項伯收九江兵盡殺布妻子布使者頗得故人幸臣將眾數千人歸漢漢益分布兵而與俱北收兵至成皋四年七月立布為淮南王與擊項籍漢五年布使人入九江得數縣六年布與劉賈入九江誘大司馬周殷周殷反楚遂舉九江兵與

漢擊楚破之垓下項籍死天下定上置酒上折隨何之功謂何爲腐儒爲天下安用腐儒索隱曰腐音輔謂之腐儒者言如腐敗之物不任用也隨何跪曰夫陛下引兵攻彭城楚王未去齊也陛下發步卒五萬人騎五千能以取淮南乎上曰不能隨何曰陛下使何與二十人使淮南至如陛下之意是何之功賢於步卒五萬人騎五千也然而陛下謂何腐儒爲天下安用腐儒何也上曰吾方圖子之功迺以隨何爲護軍中尉布遂剖符爲淮南王都六九江廬江衡山豫章郡皆屬布七年朝陳八年朝

雒陽九年朝長安十一年高后誅淮陰侯布因心恐夏漢誅梁王彭越醢之盛其醢徧賜諸侯至淮南淮南王方獵見醢因大恐陰令人部聚兵候伺旁郡警急張晏曰欲有所會布所幸姬疾請就醫醫家與中大夫賁赫對門徐廣曰賁音肥○索隱曰人姓名也姬數如醫家賁赫自以爲侍中迺厚餽遺從姬飲醫家姬侍王從容語次譽赫長者也王怒曰汝安從知之具說狀王疑其與亂赫恐稱病王愈怒欲捕赫赫言變事乘傳詣長安布使人追不及赫至上變言布謀反有端可先未發誅也上讀

其書語蕭相國相國曰布不宜有此恐仇怨妄誣之請繫赫使人微一作徵驗淮南王淮南王布見赫以罪亡上變固已疑其言國陰事漢使又來頗有所驗遂族赫家發兵反反書聞上迺赦賁赫以爲將軍上召諸將問曰布反爲之奈何皆曰發兵擊之坑豎子耳何能爲乎汝陰侯滕公召故楚令尹問之令尹曰是固當反滕公曰上裂地而王之疏爵而貴之漢書音義曰疏分也禹決江疏河是也○索隱曰尚書曰列爵惟五分土惟三按列裂地是對文故知疏即分也南面而立萬乘之主其反何也令尹曰往年殺彭越前年殺韓信張晏曰往年前年同耳使文相避也言此三人者同功一體之人也自疑禍及身故反耳滕公言之上曰臣客故楚令尹薛公者其人有籌筴之計可問上迺召見問薛公薛公對曰布反不足怪也使布出於上計山東非漢之有也出於中計勝敗之數未可知也出於下計陛下安枕而臥矣上曰何謂上計令尹對曰東取吳正義曰荊王劉賈都吳蘇州闔閭城也西取楚正義曰楚王劉交都徐州下邳并齊取魯傳檄燕趙固守其所山東非漢之有也何謂中計東取吳西取楚并韓取魏據敖倉之粟索隱曰案太康地記云秦建敖倉於成皐又立庾故亦云敖庾也塞成皐

之口勝敗之數未可知也何謂下計東取吳西取下蔡〔正義古州來國〕歸重於越身歸長沙〔正義曰今潭州〕陛下安枕而卧漢無事矣〔桓譚新論曰世有圍碁之戲或言是兵法之類也及爲之上者遠碁疏張置以會圍因而成多得道之勝中者則務相絶遮要以爭便求利故勝負狐疑須計數而定下者則守邊隅趨作罫以自生於小地然亦必不如察薛公之言上計云取吳楚并齊魯及燕趙者此廣道地之謂中計云取吳楚并韓魏塞成臯據敖倉此趨遮要爭利者也下計云取吳下蔡據長沙以臨越此守邊隅趨作罫者也○索隱曰罫音烏卦反〕上曰是計將安出令尹對曰出下計上曰何謂發上中計而出下計令尹曰布故麗山之徒也自致萬乘之主此皆爲身不顧後爲百姓萬世慮者也故曰出下計上曰善封薛公千戸〔索隱曰劉氏云薛公得封千戸蓋關内侯也〕迺立皇子長爲淮南王上遂發兵自將東擊布布之初反謂其將曰上老矣厭兵必不能來使諸將諸將獨患淮陰彭越今皆已死餘不足畏也故遂反果如薛公籌之東擊荆荆王劉賈走死富陵〔正義曰故城在楚州盱眙縣東北六十里〕盡劫其兵渡淮擊楚楚發兵與戰徐僮閒〔如淳曰地名也○索隱曰案地理志臨淮有徐縣僮縣○正義曰杜預云徐在下邳僮縣東括地志云大徐城在泗州徐城縣北四十里古徐國也〕爲三軍欲以相救爲奇或説楚將曰布善用兵民素畏之且兵法諸侯戰其地爲散地〔漢書音義曰謂散滅之地○正義曰魏武帝注孫子曰卒戀土地道近而易敗散〕今別爲三彼敗吾一軍餘

皆走安能相救不聽布果破其一軍其二軍散走遂西與上兵遇蘄西會甀索隱曰上古外反下持瑞反韋昭云蘄之鄉名漢書作㽉應劭音保非也○正義曰蘄音機沛郡蘄城也甀遂瑞反布兵精甚上乃壁庸城鄧展曰地名也望布軍置陳如項籍軍上惡之與布相望見遥謂布曰何苦而反布曰欲為帝耳上怒罵之遂大戰布軍敗走渡淮數止戰不利與百餘人走江南布故與番君婚以故長沙哀王徐廣曰表云成王臣吳芮之子也駰案晉灼曰芮之孫固或曰是成王非哀王也傳誤也使人紿布僞與亡誘走越故信而隨之番陽索隱曰番陽鄱縣之鄉番陽人殺布茲鄉民田舍正義曰英布冢在饒州鄱陽縣北百五十二里十三步

遂滅黥布立皇子長為淮南王封賁赫為期思侯正義曰期思故城在光州固始縣界諸將率多以功封者漢書曰將封者六人

太史公曰英布者其先豈春秋所見楚滅英六皐陶之後哉身被刑法何其拔興之暴也索隱曰拔音白皃反疾也項氏之所坑殺人以千萬數而布常為首虐功冠諸侯用此得王亦不免於身為世大僇禍之興自愛姬殖妒媢生患竟以滅國媢音冒媢亦妒也○索隱曰漢書外戚傳亦云成結寵妾妬媢之誅又論衡云妬夫媢婦則媢是妬之別名今原英布之誅為疑賁赫與其姬妃有亂故至滅國所以不得言妬媢是媢也一云男妬曰媢

索隱述贊曰

九江初筮　當刑而王　旣免徒中
聚盜江上　每雄楚卒　頻破秦將
病爲羽疑　歸受漢杖　賁赫見毀
卒致無妄

黥布列傳第三十一　史記九十一

淮陰侯列傳第三十二　　史記九十二

淮陰侯韓信者淮陰人也正義曰楚州淮陰縣也始爲布衣時貧無行不得推擇爲吏李奇曰無善行可推舉選擇又不能治生商賈常從人寄食飲人多厭之者常數從其下鄉南昌亭長寄食張晏曰下鄉縣屬淮陰也○索隱曰案楚漢春秋南昌作新昌亭長者主亭之吏也數月亭長妻患之乃晨炊蓐食張晏曰未起而牀蓐中食食時信往不爲具食信亦知其意怒竟絕去信釣於城下正義曰淮陰城北臨淮水昔信去下鄉而釣於此諸母漂韋昭曰以水擊絮爲漂故曰漂母有一母見信飢飯信竟漂數十日信喜謂漂母曰吾必有以重報母母怒曰大

丈夫不能自食正義音寺吾哀王孫而進食蘇林曰如言公子也○索隱曰劉德曰秦末多失國言王孫公子尊之也張晏云字王孫非也豈望報乎淮陰屠中少年有侮信者曰若雖長大好帶刀劒中情怯耳衆辱之曰信能死刺我不能死出我袴下徐廣曰袴一作胯胯股也音同又云漢書作跨同耳○索隱曰胯音枯化反然尋此文作袴欲依字讀何爲不通袴下即胯下也何必須要作胯下於是信孰視之俛出袴下蒲伏正義俛音俛伏蒲北反一市人皆笑信以爲怯及項梁渡淮信杖劒從之居戲下徐廣曰戲一作麾無所知名項梁敗又屬項羽羽以爲郎中數以策干項羽羽不用漢王之入蜀信亡楚歸漢未得知名爲連敖徐廣曰典

客也○索隱曰李奇云楚官名張晏曰司馬也坐法當斬其輩十三人皆已斬次至信信乃仰視適見滕公曰上不欲就天下乎何爲斬壯士滕公奇其言壯其貌釋而不斬與語大説之言於上上拜以爲治粟都尉上未之奇也信數與蕭何語何奇之至南鄭諸將行道亡者數十人信度何等已數言上上不我用即亡何聞信亡不及以聞自追之人有言上曰丞相何亡上大怒如失左右手居一二日何來謁上上且怒且喜罵何曰若亡何也何曰臣不敢亡也臣追亡者上曰若所追者誰何曰韓

信也上復罵曰諸將亡者以十數公無所追追信詐也何曰諸將易得耳至如信者國士無雙王必欲長王漢中無所事信文穎曰事猶業也張晏曰無事用信必欲爭天下非信無所與計事者顧王策安所決耳王曰吾亦欲東耳安能鬱鬱久居此乎何曰王計必欲東能用信信即留不能用信信終亡耳王曰吾爲公以爲將何曰雖爲將信必不留王曰以爲大將何曰幸甚於是王欲召信拜之何曰王素慢無禮今拜大將如呼小兒耳此乃信所以去也王必欲拜之擇良日齋戒設壇場具

禮乃可耳王許之諸將皆喜人人各自以爲得大將至拜大將乃韓信也一軍皆驚信拜禮畢上坐王曰丞相數言將軍將軍何以教寡人計策信謝因問王曰今東鄉爭權天下豈非項王耶漢王曰然曰大王自料勇悍仁彊孰與項王漢王默然良久曰不如也信再拜賀曰惟信亦爲大王不如也然臣嘗事之請言項王之爲人也項王喑噁叱咤千人皆發（晉灼曰發不收也○索隱曰喑於鴆反噁烏路反叱昌栗反咤卓嫁反咤或作吒喑噁懷怒氣叱咤發怒聲孟康曰發廢狀也張晏曰廢偃也）然不能任屬賢將此特匹夫之勇耳項王見人恭敬慈

愛言語嘔嘔（音凶于反○索隱曰嘔音吁嘔嘔猶區區也漢書作姁姁鄧展曰姁姁和好貌也）人有疾病涕泣分食飲至使人有功當封爵者印刓弊忍不能予（漢書音義曰不忍授）此所謂婦人之仁也項王雖霸天下而臣諸侯不居關中而都彭城有背義帝之約而以親愛王諸侯不平諸侯之見項王遷逐義帝置江南亦皆歸逐其主而自王善地項王所過無不殘滅者天下多怨百姓不親附特劫於威彊耳名雖爲霸實失天下心故曰其彊易弱今大王誠能反其道任天下武勇何所不誅以天下城邑封功臣何所不服以

義兵從思東歸之士何所不散索隱曰劉氏云用東歸之兵擊東方之敵此敵無不散敗也且三秦王爲秦將將秦子弟數歲矣所殺亡不可勝計又欺其衆降諸侯至新安項王詐坑秦降卒二十餘萬唯獨邯欣翳得脫秦父兄怨此三人痛入骨髓今楚彊以威王此三人秦民莫愛也大王之入武關秋豪無所害索隱曰案秋豪家秋乃成王逸注楚詞云銳毛爲豪夏落秋生也除秦苛法與秦民約法三章耳秦民無不欲得大王王秦者於諸侯之約大王當王關中關中民咸知之大王失職入漢中秦民無不恨者今大王舉而東三秦可傳檄

而定也索隱曰案說文云檄二尺書也此云傳檄謂爲檄書以責所伐者於是漢王大喜自以爲得信晚遂聽信計部署諸將所擊八月漢王舉兵東出陳倉正義曰漢王從關北出岐州陳倉縣定三秦漢二年出關正義曰出函谷關收魏河南韓殷王皆降合齊趙共擊楚四月至彭城漢兵敗散而還信復收兵與漢王會滎陽復擊破楚京索之閒以故楚兵卒不能西漢之敗卻彭城正義曰兵敗散彭城而卻退塞王欣翟王翳亡漢降楚齊趙亦反漢與楚和六月魏王豹謁歸視親疾至國即絕河關索隱曰今蒲津關反漢與楚約和漢王使酈生說豹不下其八月

以信爲左丞相擊魏魏王盛兵蒲坂塞臨晉索隱曰塞音先得反臨晉縣名在河東之東岸對舊關也信乃益爲疑兵漢書音義曰益張旌旗以疑敵者陳船欲渡臨晉索隱曰劉氏云陳船地名在舊關之西今之朝邑非也案京兆有船司空縣不名陳船陳船者陳列船艘欲渡河也而伏兵從夏陽以木罌缻渡軍徐廣曰缻一作缶服虔曰以木押縛罌缻以渡韋昭曰以木爲器如罌缻以渡軍無船且尚密也○正義曰按韓信詐陳列船艘於臨晉欲渡河即此從夏陽木押罌缻度軍襲安邑臨晉同州東朝邑界夏陽在同州北渭城界襲安邑正義曰安邑故城在絳州夏縣東北十五里魏王豹驚引兵迎信信遂虜豹索隱曰劉氏云夏陽舊無船豹不備之而防臨晉耳今安邑被襲故豹遂降也定魏爲河東郡正義曰理安邑縣故城漢王遣張耳與信俱引兵東北擊趙代後九月破代兵禽夏說閼與徐廣曰音

余駰案李奇曰夏說代相也○索隱曰司馬彪郡國志上黨沾縣有閼與聚閼音曷又音焉與音余又音預沾音他廉反○正義曰閼與聚城在潞州銅鞮縣西北二十里信之下魏破代漢輒使人收其精兵詣滎陽以距楚信與張耳以兵數萬欲東下井陘擊趙索隱曰案地理志常山石邑縣井陘山在西又穆天子傳云至于陘山之隧升于三道之磴是也趙王成安君陳餘聞漢且襲之也聚兵井陘口正義曰井陘故關在并州石艾縣陘東十八里即井陘口號稱二十萬廣武君李左車說成安君曰聞漢將韓信涉西河虜魏王禽夏說新喋血閼與索隱曰喋舊音鈙非也案陳湯傳喋血萬里之外如淳云殺人血流滂沲也韋昭音徒協反今乃輔以張耳議欲下趙此乘勝而去國遠鬬其鋒不可當臣聞千里

餽糧士有飢色樵蘇後爨漢書音義曰樵取薪也蘇取草也師不宿飽今井陘之道車不得方軌騎不得成列行數百里其勢糧食必在其後願足下假臣奇兵三萬人從閒路絕其輜重足下深溝高壘堅營勿與戰彼前不得鬬退不得還吾奇兵絕其後使野無所掠不至十日而兩將之頭可致於戲下願君留意臣之計不必爲二子所禽矣成安君儒者也常稱義兵不用詐謀奇計曰吾聞兵法十則圍之倍則戰之今韓信兵號數萬其實不過數千能千里而襲我亦已罷極今如此避

而不擊後有大者何以加之則諸侯謂吾怯而輕來伐我不聽廣武君策廣武君策不用韓信使人閒視知其不用還報則大喜乃敢引兵遂下正義曰引兵入井陘狹道出趙未至井陘口三十里止舍夜半傳發漢書音義曰傳令軍中使發選輕騎二千人人持一赤幟從閒道萆山而望趙軍如淳曰萆音蔽依山自覆蔽○索隱曰案謂令從閒道小路向前望見陳餘軍營即住仍須隱山自蔽勿令趙軍知也蔽者蓋覆也楚漢春秋作卑山漢書作萆說文云萆蔽也從甲竹聲誡曰趙見我走必空壁逐我若疾入趙壁拔趙幟立漢赤幟令其裨將傳飱徐廣曰音飡食也○索隱曰如淳曰小飯曰飡謂立駐傳飡食待破趙乃大食也曰今日破趙會食服虔曰立駐傳飡食也如

淳曰小飯曰飡言破趙後乃當共飽食也諸將皆莫信詳應曰諾謂軍吏曰趙已先據便地爲壁且彼未見吾大將旗鼓未肯擊前行恐吾至阻險而還信乃使萬人先行出背水陳正義曰綿蔓水一名阜將一名洄星自井州流入井陘界即信背水陣陷之死地即此水也趙軍望見而大笑平旦信建大將之旗鼓鼓行出井陘口趙開壁擊之正義曰恒州鹿泉縣即六國時趙壁也大戰良久於是信張耳詳棄鼓旗走水上軍水上軍開入之復疾戰趙果空壁爭漢鼓旗逐韓信張耳韓信張耳已入水上軍軍皆殊死戰不可敗信所出奇兵二千騎共候趙空壁逐利則馳

入趙壁皆拔趙旗立漢赤幟二千趙軍已不勝不能得信等欲還歸壁壁皆漢赤幟而大驚以爲漢皆已得趙王將矣兵遂亂遁走趙將雖斬之不能禁也於是漢兵夾擊大破虜趙軍斬成安君泜水上禽趙王歇信乃令軍中毋殺廣武君有能生得者購千金於是有縛廣武君而致戲下者信乃解其縛東鄉坐西鄉對師事之諸將効首虜索隱曰如淳云効致也晉灼曰効數也鄭玄注禮効猶呈見也休畢賀因問信曰兵法右倍山陵前左水澤今者將軍令臣等反背水陳曰破趙會食臣等不服然竟以勝

此何術也信曰此在兵法顧諸君不察耳兵法不曰陷之死地而後生置之亡地而後存且信非得素拊循士大夫也此所謂驅市人而戰之其勢非置之死地使人人自為戰今予之生地皆走寧尚可得而用之乎諸將皆服曰善非臣所及也於是信問廣武君曰僕欲北攻燕東伐齊何若而有功廣武君辭謝曰臣聞敗軍之將不可以言勇亡國之大夫不可以圖存今臣敗亡之虜何足以權大事乎信曰僕聞之百里奚居虞而虞亡在秦而秦霸非愚於虞而智於秦

也用與不用聽與不聽也誠令成安君聽足下計若信者亦已為禽矣以不用足下故信得侍耳因固問曰僕委心歸計願足下勿辭廣武君曰臣聞智者千慮必有一失愚者千慮必有一得故曰狂夫之言聖人擇焉顧恐臣計未必足用願效愚忠夫成安君有百戰百勝之計一旦而失之軍敗鄗下李奇曰鄗音臛今高邑是身死泜上今將軍涉西河索隱曰此之西河當馮翊也○正義曰即同州龍門河從夏陽度者虜魏王禽夏說閼與一舉而下井陘不終朝破趙二十萬衆誅成安君名聞海內威震天下農夫莫敢輟

耕釋耒褕衣甘食索隱曰褕鄒氏音瑜美也恐滅亡不日以故廢止作業而事美衣甘食一曰偷苟且也慮不圖久故也漢書作美衣媮食傾耳以待命者如淳曰恐滅亡不久故也若此將軍之所長也然而衆勞卒罷其實難用今將軍欲舉倦弊之兵頓之燕堅城之下欲戰恐久力不能拔情見勢屈曠日糧竭而弱燕不服齊必竟以自彊也燕齊相持而不下則劉項之權未有所分也若此者將軍所短也臣愚竊以為亦過矣故善用兵者不以短擊長而以長擊短韓信曰然則何由廣武君對曰方今為將軍計莫如案甲休兵鎮趙撫其孤百里之內牛酒

日至以饗士大夫醳兵魏都賦曰青醳順時劉逵曰醳酒也○索隱曰劉氏依劉逵作醳酒謂以酒食養兵士也案史記古釋字皆如此豈亦謂以酒食醳兵士故字從酉乎北首燕路正義曰首音狩向也而後遣辯士奉咫尺之書正義曰咫尺八寸言其簡牘或長尺也暴其所長於燕正義曰暴音僕燕必不敢不聽從燕已從使諠言者東告齊齊必從風而服雖有智者亦不知為齊計矣如是則天下事皆可圖也兵固有先聲而後實者此之謂也韓信曰善從其策發使使燕燕從風而靡乃遣使報漢因請立張耳為趙王以鎮撫其國漢王許之乃立張耳為趙王楚數奇兵渡河擊趙趙王耳韓信往

來救趙因行定趙城邑發兵詣漢漢王於滎陽漢王南出之宛葉間[正義曰宛在鄧州葉在許州]得黥布走入城皐楚又復急圍之六月漢王出城皐東渡河獨與滕公俱從張耳軍脩武至宿傳舍晨自稱漢使馳入趙壁張耳韓信未起即其卧內上奪其印符以麾召諸將易置之信耳起乃知漢王來大驚漢王奪兩人軍即令張耳備守趙地拜韓信爲相國收趙兵未發者擊齊[文穎曰謂趙人未嘗見發者]信引兵東未渡平原[正義曰懷州有平原津]聞漢王使酈食其已說下齊韓信欲止范陽辯士蒯

通說信曰將軍受詔擊齊而漢獨發間使下齊寧有詔止將軍乎何以得毋行也且酈生一士伏軾[韋昭曰軾今小車中隆起者]掉三寸之舌下齊七十餘城將軍將數萬衆歲餘乃下趙五十餘城爲將數歲反不如一豎儒之功乎於是信然之從其計遂渡河齊已聽生即留縱酒罷備漢守禦信因襲齊歷下軍[徐廣曰齊南歷城縣]遂至臨菑齊王田廣以酈生賣己乃亨之而走高密使使之楚請救韓信已定臨菑遂東追廣至高密西楚亦使龍且將號稱二十萬救齊齊王廣龍且并軍與信戰未

合人或說龍且曰漢兵遠鬬窮戰其鋒不可當齊楚自居其地戰兵易敗散正義曰近其室家懷顧望也不如深壁令齊王使其信臣招所亡城亡城聞其王在楚來救必反漢漢兵二千里客居齊城皆反之其勢無所得食可無戰而降也龍且曰吾平生知韓信爲人易與耳且夫救齊不戰而降之吾何功今戰而勝之齊之半可得何爲止遂戰與信夾濰水陳徐廣曰出東莞而東北流至北海都昌縣入海○索隱曰濰音維地理志濰水出琅邪箕縣東北至昌都入海徐所引蓋據水經與此小不同韓信乃夜令人爲萬餘囊滿盛沙壅水上流引軍半渡擊龍且佯不勝還走龍且果喜曰固知信怯也遂追渡水信使人決壅囊水大至龍且軍大半不得渡即急擊殺龍且龍且水東軍散走齊王廣亡去信遂追北至城陽正義曰城陽雷澤縣是也在濮州東南九十一里皆虜楚卒漢四年遂皆降平齊使人言漢王曰齊僞詐多變反覆之國也南邊楚不爲假王以鎮之其勢不定願爲假王便當是時楚方急圍漢王於滎陽韓信使者至發書張晏曰發信使者所齎書漢王大怒罵曰吾困於此旦暮望若來佐我乃欲自立爲王張良陳平躡漢王足因附耳語曰漢方不利寧能禁

信之王乎不如因而立善遇之使自爲守不然變生漢王亦悟因復罵曰大丈夫定諸侯即爲眞王耳何以假爲乃遣張良往立信爲齊王（徐廣曰四年二月）徵其兵擊楚楚已亡龍且項王恐使盱眙人武涉（張華曰武涉墓在盱眙城東十五里）往說齊王信曰天下共苦秦久矣相與戮力擊秦秦已破計功割地分土而王之以休士卒今漢王復興兵而東侵人之分奪人之地已破三秦引兵出關收諸侯之兵以東擊楚其意非盡吞天下者不休其不知厭足如是甚也且漢王不可必身居項王掌握

中數矣（正義曰數色角反）項王憐而活之然得脫輒倍約復擊項王其不可親信如此今足下雖自以與漢王爲厚交爲之盡力用兵終爲之所禽矣足下所以得須臾至今者以項王尚存也當今二王之事權在足下足下右投則漢王勝左投則項王勝項王今日亡則次取足下足下與項王有故何不反漢與楚連和參分天下王之今釋此時而自必於漢以擊楚且爲智者固若此乎韓信謝曰臣事項王官不過郎中位不過執戟（張晏曰郎中宿衛執戟之人也）言不聽畫不用故倍楚而歸漢漢

王授我上將軍印予我數萬衆解衣衣我推食
食我言聽計用故吾得以至於此夫人深親信
我我倍之不祥雖死不易幸爲信謝項王武涉
已去齊人蒯通知天下權在韓信欲爲奇策而
感動之以相人說韓信曰僕嘗受相人之術韓
信曰先生相人何如對曰貴賤在於骨法憂喜
在於容色成敗在於決斷以此參之萬不失一
韓信曰善先生相寡人何如對曰願少閒信曰
左右去矣通曰相君之面不過封矦又危不安
相君之背貴乃不可言張晏曰背畔則大貴韓信曰何謂

也蒯通曰天下初發難也俊雄豪傑建號壹呼
天下之士雲合霧集魚鱗雜遝熛至風起當此
之時憂在亡秦而已今楚漢分爭使天下無罪
之人肝膽塗地父子暴骸骨於中野不可勝數
楚人起彭城轉鬬逐北至於滎陽乘利席卷威
震天下然兵困於京索之閒迫西山而不能進
者三年於此矣漢王將數十萬之衆距鞏雒阻
山河之險一日數戰無尺寸之功折北不救張晏曰折衄敗也北奔北也
敗滎陽傷城皋張晏曰於城皋傷胷也呂靜曰謂軍折傷遂走
宛葉之閒此所謂智勇俱困者也夫銳氣挫於

險塞而糧食竭於內府百姓罷極怨望容容無所倚以臣料之其勢非天下之賢聖固不能息天下之禍當今兩主之命縣於足下足下為漢則漢勝與楚則楚勝臣願披腹心輸肝膽效愚計恐足下不能用也誠能聽臣之計莫若兩利而俱存之參分天下鼎足而居其勢莫敢先動夫以足下之賢聖有甲兵之衆據彊齊從燕趙出空虛之地而制其後因民之欲西鄉（正義曰鄉音向齊國在東故曰西向也）為百姓請命（正義曰止楚漢之戰鬬士卒之命故云請命）則天下風走而響應矣孰敢不聽割大弱彊以立諸侯諸

侯已立天下服聽而歸德於齊案齊之故有膠泗之地懷諸侯之德深拱揖讓則天下之君王相率而朝於齊矣蓋聞天與弗取反受其咎時至不行反受其殃願足下孰慮之韓信曰漢王遇我甚厚載我以其車衣我以其衣食我以其食吾聞之乘人之車者載人之患衣人之衣者懷人之憂食人之食者死人之事吾豈可以鄉利倍義乎蒯生曰足下自以為善漢王欲建萬世之業臣竊以為誤矣始常山王成安君為布衣時相與為刎頸之交後爭張黶陳澤之事二

人相怨常山王背項王奉項嬰頭而竄逃歸於
漢王漢王借兵而東下殺成安君泜水之南頭
足異處卒為天下笑此二人相與天下至驩也
然而卒相禽者何也患生於多欲而人心難測
也今足下欲行忠信以交於漢王必不能固於
二君之相與也而事多大於張黶陳澤故臣以
為足下必漢王之不危己亦誤矣大夫種范蠡
存亡越霸句踐立功成名而身死亡野獸已盡
而獵狗亨夫以交友言之則不如張耳之與成
安君者也以忠信言之則不過大夫種范蠡之

於句踐也此二人者足以觀矣願足下深慮之
且臣聞勇略震主者身危而功蓋天下者不賞
臣請言大王功略足下涉西河虜魏王禽夏說
引兵下井陘誅成安君徇趙脅燕定齊南摧楚
人之兵二十萬東殺龍且西鄉以報此所謂功
無二於天下而略不世出者也今足下戴震主
之威挾不賞之功歸楚楚人不信歸漢漢人震
恐足下欲持是安歸乎夫勢在人臣之位而有
震主之威名高天下竊為足下危之韓信謝曰
先生且休矣吾將念之後數日蒯通復說曰夫

聽者事之候也計者事之機也聽過計失而能久安者鮮矣聽不失一二者不可亂以言計不失本末者不可紛以辭夫隨厮養之役者失萬乘之權守儋石之祿者晉灼曰揚雄方言海岱之間名罌爲儋石斗石也蘇林曰齊人名小罌爲儋石如今受鮎魚石罌不過一二石耳一說一儋與一斛之餘○索隱曰儋音都濫反石斗也蘇林解爲得之鮎音胎闕卿相之位故知者決之斷也疑者事之害也審豪氂之小計遺天下之大數智誠知之決弗敢行者百事之禍也故曰猛虎之猶豫不若蜂蠆之致螫正義音適騏驥之跼躅徐廣曰跼一作蹢也不如駑馬之安步孟賁之狐疑不如庸夫之必至也

雖有舜禹之智吟而不言不如瘖聾之指麾也索隱曰鄒氏吟音巨蔭反又音琴此言貴能行之夫功者難成而易敗時者難得而易失也時乎時不再來願足下詳察之韓信猶豫不忍倍漢又自以爲功多漢終不奪我齊遂謝蒯通蒯通說不聽已詳狂爲巫徐廣曰一本遂不用蒯通蒯通曰夫迫於細苛者不可與圖大事拘於臣虜者固無君王之意說不聽因去詳狂也○索隱曰案漢書及戰國策皆有此文漢王之困固陵用張良計召齊王信遂將兵會垓下項羽已破高祖襲奪齊王軍徐廣曰以齊爲平原千乘東萊齊郡漢五年正月徙齊王信爲楚王都下邳信至國召所從食漂母賜千金

（張華曰漂母冢在泗口南岸）及下鄉南昌亭長賜百錢曰公小
人也爲德不卒召辱己之少年令出胯下者以
爲楚中尉告諸將相曰此壯士也方辱我時我
寧不能殺之邪殺之無名故忍而就於此項王
亡將鍾離眛家在伊廬（徐廣曰東海朐縣有伊廬鄉駰案韋昭曰今中廬縣○索隱曰徐注出司馬彪郡國志○正義曰括地志云中廬在義清縣北二十里本春秋時廬戎之國也秦謂之伊廬漢爲中廬縣項羽之將鍾離眛冢在焉韋昭及括地志云皆說之也）素與信善項王死後亡
歸信漢王怨眛聞其在楚詔楚捕眛信初之國
行縣邑陳兵出入漢六年人有上書告楚王信
反高帝以陳平計天子巡狩會諸侯南方有雲

夢發使告諸侯會陳吾將游雲夢實欲襲信信
弗知高祖且至楚信欲發兵反自度無罪欲謁
上恐見禽人或說信曰斬眛謁上上必喜無患
信見眛計事眛曰漢所以不擊取楚以眛在公
所若欲捕我以自媚於漢吾今日死公亦隨手
亡矣乃罵信曰公非長者卒自剄信持其首謁
高祖於陳上令武士縛信載後車信曰果若人
言狡兔死良狗亨（張晏曰狡猶猾○索隱曰吳越春秋作郊兔戰國策曰東郭逡海內狡兔也）高鳥盡良弓藏敵國破謀臣亡天下已定我
固當亨上曰人告公反遂械繫信至雒陽赦信

罪以爲淮陰侯信知漢王畏惡其能常稱病不朝從信由此日怨望居常鞅鞅羞與絳灌等列信常過樊將軍噲噲跪拜送迎言稱臣曰大王乃肯臨臣信出門笑曰生乃與噲等爲伍上常從容與信言諸將能不各有差上問曰如我能將幾何信曰陛下不過能將十萬上曰於君何如曰臣多多而益善耳上笑曰多多益善何爲爲我禽信曰陛下不能將兵而善將將此乃信之所以爲陛下禽也且陛下所謂天授非人力也陳豨拜爲鉅鹿守徐廣曰表云爲趙相國將兵守代也辭於淮陰侯

淮陰侯挈其手辟左右與之步於庭仰天歎曰子可與言乎欲與子有言也豨曰唯將軍令之淮陰侯曰公所居天下精兵處也而公陛下之信幸臣也人言公之畔陛下必不信再至陛下乃疑矣三至必怒而自將吾爲公從中起天下可圖也陳豨素知其能也信之曰謹奉教漢十一年陳豨果反上自將而往信病不從陰使人至豨所曰弟舉兵吾從此助公信乃謀與家臣夜詐詔赦諸官徒奴欲發以襲呂后太子部署已定待豨報其舍人得罪於信索隱曰案晉灼曰楚漢春秋云謝公

也姚氏案功臣表云慎陽侯樂說淮陰舍人告信反者未知孰是信因欲殺之舍人弟上變告信欲反狀於呂后呂后欲召恐其黨不就乃與蕭相國謀詐令人從上所來言豨已得死列侯羣臣皆賀相國紿信曰雖疾彊入賀信入呂后使武士縛信斬之長樂鍾室正義曰長樂宮縣鍾之室信方斬之曰吾悔不用蒯通之計乃爲兒女子所詐豈非天哉遂夷信三族高祖已從豨軍來至見信死且喜且憐之問信死亦何言呂后曰信言恨不用蒯通計高祖曰是齊辯士也乃詔齊捕蒯通蒯通至上曰若教淮陰侯反乎對曰

然臣固教之豎子不用臣之策故令自夷於此如彼豎子用臣之計陛下安得而夷之乎上怒曰亨之通曰嗟乎寃哉亨也上曰若教韓信反何寃對曰秦之綱絶而維弛山東大擾異姓並起英俊烏集秦失其鹿天下共逐之張晏曰以鹿喻帝位也於是高材疾足者先得焉跖之狗吠堯堯非不仁狗固吠非其主當是時臣唯獨知韓信非知陛下也且天下鋭精持鋒欲爲陛下所爲者甚衆顧力不能耳又可盡亨之邪高帝曰置之乃釋通之罪

太史公曰吾如淮陰淮陰人爲余言韓信雖爲布衣時其志與衆異其母死貧無以葬然乃行營高敞地令其旁可置萬家余視其母冢良然假令韓信學道謙讓不伐己功不矜其能則庶幾哉於漢家勳可以比周召太公之徒後世血食矣不務出此而天下已集乃謀畔逆夷滅宗族不亦宜乎

索隱述贊曰

君臣一體　自古所難　相國深薦
策拜登壇　沉沙決水　拔幟傳飡
與漢漢重　歸楚楚安　三分不議
僞遊可歎

淮陰侯列傳第三十二　史記九十二